DATE DUE

AUG 2 6 1998			

THE HARMONY SOCIETY.

AMS PRESS
NEW YORK

THE

HARMONY SOCIETY,

AT

ECONOMY, PENN'A.

FOUNDED BY GEORGE RAPP, A. D. 1805.

WITH AN APPENDIX.

BY

AARON WILLIAMS, D. D.

PITTSBURGH:

PRINTED BY W. S. HAVEN, COR. WOOD AND THIRD STS.

1866.

459063

Reprinted from the edition of 1866, Pittburgh
First AMS edition published in 1971
Manufactured in the United States of America

International Standard Book Number:0-404-08478-8

Library of Congress Catalog Card Number:70-134412

AMS PRESS INC.
NEW YORK, N. Y. 10003

PREFATORY NOTE.

——o——

THE following Chapters, except the Introduction, originally appeared as a series of articles in the *Pittsburgh Commercial*. The first one was written in reply to a slanderous article in the *Atlantic Monthly*, entitled "The Harmonists." The others had no reference to that article, but were intended as a more full account of some of the topics cursorily noticed in the first chapter, together with an outline of the later history of the Society. The articles attracted much notice as they successively appeared, on account of the authentic information which they gave on many points about which the public generally were laboring under misapprehension. They have been enlarged and corrected, and are published in the present form at the request of many readers, and with the approbation of the Society, as will appear from the note which is found on the preceding page.

The opportunities which the writer has enjoyed for becoming acquainted with the history of the Society, have been peculiarly favorable. After a fire, by which he was summarily ejected from the Edgeworth Seminary, in February, 1865, he and his family were hospitably received at Economy, and have since been permitted to reside there. To a previous acquaintance of many years' standing, there has been added the opportunity of personal observation and of the most frank and full communication with the leaders and others, on all points pertaining to their history, opinions, &c.

He has had the use, also, of certain fragmentary memoranda prepared by one of the leaders a few years ago, on

PREFATORY NOTE.

several of the topics treated in these chapters. He has simply aimed to write as a faithful historian, without indicating his own opinions on the matters discussed.

The writer would acknowledge also his great obligation to his learned friend, Prof. R. E. Williams, of Pittsburgh, who, though not a relative, has manifested a fraternal interest in the progress of this work, and has afforded most substantial aid in the way of translations from the German, some of which will be found in the Appendix. To him especially is the reader indebted for the extended extracts from the *Hirten-Brief* which are given. This work is highly valued by the Harmonists; and it may be interesting to the reader as a specimen of the mystical speculations of Jacob Boehm and his school. It should be read along with the introductory remarks of the translator.

ECONOMY, PA., Aug. 21, 1866.

CONTENTS.

INTRODUCTION.

DECLINE OF PIETISM—REACTION—STATE OF THINGS IN WÜRTEMBERG—FANATICAL MOVEMENTS—EMIGRATION TO RUSSIAN TARTARY—THE ZOAR COMMUNITY.

THE state of religion in Germany at the close of the 18th and beginning of the 19th century, must be understood, in order to a full appreciation of the circumstances out of which grew the movement of George Rapp and his Society of Harmonists.

The Pietism of the 17th century was a revival of true religion under the labors of Arndt, Spener, Franke, Gerhardt, and others, and was similar to the Puritanism of England during the same period. The downward tendency, however, of human nature, even at its best estate, led to a degeneracy in faith and practice among the Pietists themselves, and to a general prevalence of irreligion and immorality among the masses. The established clergy even were many of them blind guides, either being zealous bigots for the orthodoxy which they held in the letter rather than in the true spirit of a scriptural faith, or verging to the opposite extreme of skepticism in its various phases of Neology and Rationalism. The universities became hot-beds of vice and infidelity. The professors and doctors of theology taught their pupils to recognize but little difference between the inspiration of Moses and the prophets and the philosophic or poetic genius of Pythagoras, Plato, or Homer. The historic records of the Old Testament were but myths, and the miracles of the New Testament were but exaggerated statements of natural facts. The *reason* was regarded as the ultimate test of truth, and all the supernatural element in the Scriptures must be so explained away as not to conflict with it. Experimental piety was but the delusion of a weak mind. Confirmation, and a participation in the sacraments, was the privilege of all who were of suitable age, and could repeat the catechism. A Christian profession required no separation from the world; church discipline was unknown; the Sabbath, after the hours of church service, was a holiday; balls, and theatres, and gaming, were perfectly orthodox amusements, and a general looseness of morals prevailed.

In this degeneracy the clergy were in advance of the people. Among the latter some sentiments of piety were still cherished. There were those who still reverenced the Bible as the word of God, and who longed for pastors who might feed them with spiritual food rather than with husks. But such pastors were rarely to be found. Sermons were, for the most part, mere moral essays; the sacraments were but lifeless and unmeaning forms, and the few devout worshipers retired from the house of God hungry and unedified.

One of the things most offensive to the truly pious was the mutilation of the grand old hymns, in which the religious poetry of Germany so much abounds. These hymns were altogether too devotional for the cold and philosophic rationalists, and they went to work to despoil them of everything savoring of those vital doctrines which they rejected, or that was expressive of high devotional feel.ng. New hymn books were introduced into many of the churches, individual towns and churches each having their own selections.

The music also accompanying the old hymns shared the same fate with the hymns themselves. Secular and operatic music was introduced into the sanctuary. "The oratorios and cantata of the theatre and beer garden," says Hurst, "were the Sabbath accompaniments of the sermons. The masses consequently began to sing less, and the period of coldest skepticism in Germany, like similar conditions in other lands, was the season when the congregations, the common people, and children, sang least, and most drowsily."

"The church now," continues Hurst, "presented a most deplorable aspect. Philosophy had come, with its high-sounding terminology, and invaded the hallowed precincts of scriptural truth. Literature, with its captivating notes, had well nigh destroyed what was left of the old Pietistic fervor. The songs of the church were no longer images of beauty, but ghastly, repulsive skeletons. The professor's chair was but little better than a heathen tripod. The pulpit became the rostrum where the shepherdless masses were entertained with vague essays on such general terms as righteousness, human dignity, light, progress truth, and right. The peasantry received frequent and labored instructions on the raising of cattle, bees, and fruit The poets of the day were publicly recited in the temples where the Reformers had preached."

Such was the deplorable state of religion in Germany in the latter part of the 18th century. It was time that a reaction were taking place. The "enemy had come in like a flood," and it was to be expected that the "Spirit of the Lord would lift up a standard against him." There was yet a "remnant" in Israel, a "seven thousand, who had not bowed the knee to Baal." The Moravians and the Pietistic mystics were among the conservators of a spiritual Christianity during the century just closed; and the leaven of their influence was still working. The missionary spirit which distinguished the Moravian brethren kept alive the activities of religion, while its more contemplative aspects were exhibited in the lives and teaching of such men as Stilling and Lavater, who had great faith in the power of prayer, and, though entertaining many fanciful and mystical notions, united a life of devout communion with God through Jesus Christ with one of active beneficence toward men.

Among the leaders of religious thought in Germany there had been also an approximation toward a more reverential treatment of the Holy Scriptures, and a reconciliation of their profound philosophy with a true religious faith. Herder, who was at once poet, philosopher, and theologian, had his early training among the Pietists, and had imbibed the spirit of *True Christianity* from Arndt's treatise under that title. He was an enthusiastic admirer of the poetry of the Bible, and by his work on Hebrew poetry he did much to recommend the Scriptures to men of taste and genius. As a preacher and theologian, also, though not without serious defects, he was far in advance of the leading

men of his day. He boldly defended the great essential doctrines of Christianity against the prevailing
skepticism; and he also did much, both by precept and
example, to restore the dignity and purity of the pastoral office.

Jacobi also did a good work in the same direction.
He was distinguished both for piety and learning. He
urged the necessity of an inward and living faith, having its seat in the heart rather than in the understanding. He adapted his teachings to the inward spiritual
wants of men, and made light of the pretended wisdom
of the philosophers as being foolishness with God. His
views were somewhat mystical, but found a ready reception in many a soul that was thirsting for a living
religion.

Harms and Schleiermacher are also among the names
of the men who gave a new impulse, each in his way,
toward the revival of genuine Protestantism. Harms
imitated Luther by publishing ninety-five *Theses*, in
which he "proclaimed the necessity of returning to the
old Lutheran faith, and proved that the religion of
[mere] reason was worthless." He struck a terrible
blow against Rationalism, and created a profound
sensation. Schleiermacher was educated partly among
the Moravians, and chiefly at Halle. The Pietistic
influences to which he was thus subjected in his youth,
never lost their power over him. He also taught that
religion is not a mere exercise of the reason, but has its
seat in the heart and inner consciousness of man. He
was a professor in the University of Halle, and afterward in Berlin. Though far from being orthodox, he
was no Rationalist. He "based his whole theology on

a *feeling of dependence on God*." " He regarded Christ the Redeemer, not as an ideal creation of the mind, but the real historical Christ as he lived in history and still lives in the church, as the centre of Christian theology." He gave a new impulse to the religious thinking of his time in a direction favorable to a living Christianity.

The preceding statements have reference to Germany generally. But old Würtemberg (where Rapp and his movement originated) deserves special mention, as the region where more of the savor of true piety had been retained than elsewhere, and where the stoutest resistance was made to the encroachments of Rationalism in matters pertaining to faith and worship. Hagenbach mentions Bengel, Oetinger. and Crusius, as men of Würtemberg, who, " in opposition to the demonstrative, as well as negative tendency of Rationalism, gave a new direction to theology by introducing into it not only a positive, but also pietistico mystical elements. Societies for practical no less than scientific purposes were founded, in order to keep alive positive religion among the people. Thus, in the minds of many, the faith of their forefathers was preserved not only as an empty legacy, but it assumed here and there, in the form of Pietism, depth and independence, in contrast with the scholastic tendency of the age." It has been usually found that in a period of religious deterioration, the clergy and men of the higher classes are among the first to go astray, while true religion still lingers in the homes and hearts of the middle and lower classes of people. It was so in Germany, and especially in Würtemberg. Tzschirner, in his con-

tinuation of Schrökh's Church History, after speaking
of the reaction above described, and of a refined
poetico-philosophical mysticism, which had been introduced, and found favor among the educated classes,
and which had led some into the Church of Rome,
through their desire for a *cult* abounding in ceremonies,
showy, and beautified by the applications of art, then
alludes to " a coarser mysticism quite independent of
the former, which showed itself among the lower and
uncultivated classes in some portions of the Lutheran
Church." " Such religious enthusiasm," he adds,
" among the lower classes, is, however, a much less
frequent phenomenon than it was formerly; whether the
reason be that there is less general religious interest
now than in other times, or that there is more knowledge and instruction among the peasantry and mechanics; and only in old Würtemberg and in Norway
some fanatics of this sect have recently appeared."
Very much, however, of what this historian (who has
few evangelical sympathies) lightly calls enthusiasm,
was most probably the spirit of true religion as it was
retained among the masses; but which, in the absence
of an enlightened and pious ministry, was left to develop itself in various erratic forms.

The following passage may give us some idea of the
more exceptionable forms in which this spirit manifested
itself, and will show us something of the state of society in
the midst of which George Rapp commenced his humble
labors: " The beginning of Pietism and Separatism in
Würtemberg belongs to a much earlier period, and here
we can merely state that during recent years enthusiasts have continued to exist in that region, in whose

heads visions of unrestrained freedom and Chiliastic dreams were about equally mixed. Most of them were mere country people and mechanics, and as both orally and in writing they reviled the government and the clergy, they were visited with civil punishments. In some instances, however, persons of other social ranks shared in this fanaticism; for example, a clergyman did so. One Friedrich, incumbent of the parish of Winzenhausen, near Laufen, wrote a book entitled '*Faith-and-Hope Glance* of the People of God in Anti-Christian Times, drawn from the Divine Prophecies, by Irenæus U—S., in the year of Christ 1800, and dedicated to all those who are waiting for the kingdom of God,' in which he announced the speedy opening of the *one thousand years*' reign, and admonished all true disciples of Jesus, as soon as the Lord should open a door into the land of Israel, to get themselves ready, with wives and children, the old, the blind, the lame, and the crippled, and to set out for Palestine. He patched his prophecies together from misunderstood passages of the prophets and the Psalms, promised to the citizens of the new kingdom the most glorious blessings, spiritual and physical, and assured them that God himself would bring horses and camels to meet these pilgrims for Palestine, and would conduct them happily to the promised land."

"A fanatic and deceiver, named Maria Gottlieb Kummerin, of Kleebronn, in the bailiwick of Brockenheimer (who had formerly so imposed upon a credulous curate as under pretense of a divine command to lead him into a violation of the seventh commandment with herself), now contrived to use these prophecies in such a way as

to gather followers about her; and after having paid
the penalty of her roguery in the house of correction,
she concluded to emigrate; and in the year 1801 she
succeeded—mainly by appealing to the prophecies of
Friedrich—in persuading some credulous country people that the persecutions of Anti-christ were shortly to
begin in Würtemberg, and that it was advisable therefore to go to the Holy Land. Accompanied by twenty
to thirty persons from Meinsheim, Kleebronn, and
places adjacent, she set out on the journey, and wandered as far as Vienna, where the ambassador of Würtemberg, to whom she applied for a passport, arrested
her progress, and sent her and her companions home
again." For more of such "Chiliastic dreams," see
Appendix A.

Such outgrowths of folly and fanaticism were of
course confined chiefly to the lowest and most ignorant
class of people, and were calculated to bring reproach
upon the more sober millennarian views which generally
prevailed among the Bible-reading and pious people of
that day. Such an interpretation of the Scriptures
was not new, but had been handed down from the
apostolic age, and was still defended by some of the
best men of that period. Bengel and Jung Stilling
were zealous millennarians, and they endeavored to
ascertain the moment when this event would take place.
The former fixed upon the year 1836.

It may not be amiss here to add, that the revival
of this theory, within the last few years, by such men
as Dr. Cumming, Elliott, and the Bonars, in Great
Britain, and by Lord, Seiss, and many others in this
country, in connection with the general agreement

among prophetic commentators as to the fact that the signs of the last days are upon us, are circumstances which commend these views to the most respectful attention of all who reverence the word of God. Admitting that there may be serious objections, both presumptive and exegetical, against the millennarian theory of the speedy, personal, and visible advent of Christ, it cannot be denied that there is mass of Scripture testimony in its favor, if a literal interpretation is to be allowed. At any rate, Rapp and his followers, in their zealous adherence to this view, are not to be confounded with such fanatics as those above described. For a statement of their views on this subject, see Chapter VIII.

In a recent missionary journal we find an account of a certain company of laborers from the Basle Missionary Society, sent out in 1822 to Russian Tartary, whose " primary object was to revive religion among the German colonists of those regions, who, in the midst of Tartar hordes and the superstitions of corrupt churches, were in danger of losing the distinctness of reformed Christianity, and of being mingled among the heathen, and learning their ways." The following brief notice of these colonists would imply that they must have gone forth from Würtemberg about the same time, and under the same influences which led to the emigration of Rapp and his people to America: " These German colonists consisted of emigrants from Würtemberg, who, having separated from the established church of that country in consequence of some alterations in the prayers and hymns effected by the neological party, then in the ascendency, and believing that great troubles were at hand, resolved to seek an asylum in the vicinity of the Caspian Sea, and there await the speedy advent, as they hoped it would be, of the millennial period. They were joined by others desirous of change, but uninfluenced by religious motives, and, these being in the majority, prepared the way for that religious declension which the Basle missionaries were intended to counteract." For a more full account of this colony, see Appendix B.

As further indicative of the religious and social tendencies in Würtemberg at this period, may be noticed also the emigration of another colony of Separatists, which took place in 1817, under the leading of one Joseph M. Bimeler. They belonged to the same class of people with the followers of George Rapp, and entertained views very much in common with them on religious subjects. They shared also with them the name of Separatists; but they differed on the question of allegiance due to the government. Rapp had always inculcated the duty of being subject to the " powers that be," by paying taxes, performing military duty, &c. But Bimeler and his adherents denounced both state and church as constituting that " great Babylon" which was to be destroyed; and they not only separated themselves from the established church, but they abjured allegiance to the civil authorities, refused to pay taxes, or to render military service, or even to show ordinary civility to any magistrates, whether higher or lower. They thus brought upon themselves deserved civil penalties in the way of fines and imprisonment, while they shared also in the religious persecutions which Rapp and other Separatists encountered. Bimeler himself escaped imprisonment only by removing from place to place, and by living in the utmost privacy; while Johannes Goesele, another of their leaders, was imprisoned for nine years. The following characteristic anedocte is told of him and the Duke of Würtemberg:—In the stated visits of theduke to the fort where Goesele and others were confined, frequent conversations took place between them, during which Goesele, in Quaker fashion, refused to take off his hat to the duke, and always addressed him with the disrespectful *thee* and *thou* of the German, while he freely dealt out to him the denunciations of his sect against the government. The bluff but sensible old duke took all this in good part. But on one occasion, when Napoleon was making a visit to the duke, he asked to see Goesele, who had become somewhat famous. The emperor, however, received no more respectful treatment from the doughty prisoner than the duke had done, but was boldly warned of the dread account he should have to render in the great day, for the multitude of souls he was hurrying into eternity by his bloody wars. Napoleon was provoked, and desired to have the man punished for his insolence; but as soon as the emperor had gone, the duke summoned his prisoner before him, and, instead of punishing him, as he expected, he said, "Goesele, if you had not talked to the emperor just as you talked to me, I would have taken off your head, but now, since you treat us both alike, you may go home." And he was set at liberty.

Although these people gloried in suffering, as they believed, for righteousness' sake, they at length grew weary of their trials, and resolved to follow the example of Rapp and his party, by emigrating to America. They came by way of London, and both there and in Philadelphia, on their arrival in 1817, they received much sympathy from the Society of Friends, whom in some respects they resembled. They finally purchased over five thousand acres of land in Tuscarawas county, Ohio, the same tract that George Rapp had visited some thirteen years before, while seeking a location for his colony. Here they formed their settlement, on the same general plan with that of Rapp and the Harmonists. They practiced celibacy from the first, but it was some two years later before they organized themselves on the principle of community of goods. Their town was named Zoar. Their industry, frugality, good morals, and harmonious co-operation, were similar to those of Rapp's people, and were crowned with the same rewards by a rapid increase in wealth and prosperity.

In 1852, their property was estimated to be worth over a million of dollars. They own over 10,000 acres of land, and are largely engaged in agriculture and manufactures. About the year 1832, in order to prevent the further diminution of their numbers (which did not exceed 150), they abandoned celibacy, Bimeler himself setting the example of taking a wife. The example was readily followed by all, except a few faithful ones, who were indignant at this departure from their primitive faith and practice. Although the Zoar Society seems thus to be likely to outlive that of the Economites, where celibacy is still adhered to, yet it is doubtful whether the increasing ascendency of the American born element among them will not in a very few years lead to an abandonment of the community system and a dissolution of the society. For a further notice of the Zoar community, see Appendix B.

The reader who may desire to know something of the style of religious thought which characterized the mystics and mystico-pietists to whom allusion is often made in these pages, may find it in Appendix F.

THE HARMONY SOCIETY.

───────── • ❖ • ─────────

[THE first chapter was introduced to the readers of the
Pittsburgh *Commercial* by the following editorial remarks,
under date of June 6th, 1866:

"THE HARMONY SOCIETY AT ECONOMY, PA.—We take
pleasure in calling the attention of our readers to the article
in our columns under this caption. The information it contains will be new to many, and must serve to remove misapprehensions which exist in regard to a people so well
known, and yet so little understood. The article in the
Atlantic Monthly, which is referred to by our correspondent,
must appear, in view of these statements, to be a gross
and silly caricature of the true history of the Society.

"The first inquiry that will arise in the mind of the re-
flecting reader, in view of the fact that this wealthy community must in a few years cease to exist under its present
organization, is as to what is to *become of their vast wealth?*
Their *last man* will be lord of an immense domain, but cannot live long to enjoy it, as they are now all growing
old together. We would that another 'fresh revival'
might diffuse its hallowed influences over them, so as to
prompt them to a further enlargement of their characteristic
benevolence, by providing in advance for such an investment
of their wealth, after they are done with it, as may make it
most extensively available to the good of mankind. We
would not presume to say in what way this should be done.
That is for themselves to determine. But if we had the ear

of their leaders we should be glad to suggest to them some of the many ways in which they might secure an immortality of blessedness to their memory, by providing endowments for literary, scientific, and philanthropic institutions, after the manner of Peabody and others of glorious name. And if they should reply, that the world is likely soon to come to an end, we would humbly suggest that as it has already lasted considerably longer than they expected, it may possily endure a few centuries longer still, and at any rate no harm but much good may be done by giving their posthumous wealth to some noble charities, *so long as the world shall stand.*"]

CHAPTER I.

REPLY TO THE ATLANTIC MONTHLY.

EARLY HISTORY OF THE SOCIETY—THEIR CONNECTION WITH THE EARLY PIETISTS—PERSECUTIONS IN GERMANY—REMOVAL TO AMERICA—COMMUNITY OF GOODS—CELIBACY—DEATH OF RAPP, SR.—PRESENT ORGANIZATION—BENEVOLENCE.

THE leading article in the May number of the *Atlantic Monthly*, under the caption of "The Harmonists," although intended, no doubt, as a harmless piece of romance, does very great injustice to that worthy Society, in some of its statements. There is an air of verisimilitude in the description of the place and people, which, though grossly inaccurate in the details, may convey the impression that the author was correctly informed in regard to the history and customs of the Society, and that they are verily the gross, ignorant and contemptible people which he (?) represents. This is far from being true. And although they can well afford to be misrepresented, and have never troubled themselves to refute the various slanders which have been circulated concerning them, still they cannot be wholly indifferent to the good opinion of their fellow citizens.

The writer of this has no sort of connection with the Society, except as a sojourner among them, but has had peculiarly favorable opportunities for becoming acquainted with their history, opinions, and customs; and from a regard to the truth of history, rather than from any importance attaching to the slanderous article in question, he takes this occasion to execute a purpose for some time cherished of furnishing to the public a true history of the Society. It may serve to correct some prevalent misapprehensions, and may afford interesting information in regard to a singular and most worthy people.

The Harmony Society was founded near the beginning of the present century, by George Rapp and a colony of emigrants from Würtemberg, numbering over one hundred families. Like the Pilgrim fathers, they sought this country as an asylum from oppression, and a place where they might enjoy freedom to worship God according to their understanding of his Word. They belonged to that class of devout people in Germany to whom, in the previous century, had been given in reproach the name of *Pietists*. Dissatisfied with the utter worldliness and entire absence of practical piety in the established Lutheran Church, and finding in none of the regular clergy such spiritual guides as they cared to follow, they gave themselves the more diligently to the private study of the Scriptures (a practice which they still retain), and to the edification of each other in social assemblages for conference and prayer. With an instinctive sense of their need of official teachers and guides, it was natural that they should rally around those among themselves who seemed most endowed with spiritual gifts.

There were two men who thus soon found themselves in the position of leaders, through the common consent of their brethren, though without any special ecclesiastical consecration to their work. These were Michael Hahn and George Rapp. They were earnest, zealous men, who magnified their office by gathering together on the Sabbath the people who sympathized with them, and addressing to them words of instruction and encouragement.

Hahn had commenced the work of preaching at an earlier period than Rapp. He was a man of more literary culture, and made use of the press also in the work of reformation, publishing tracts, hymns, &c. Rapp was an humble farmer and vine planter, with only such education as the common schools afforded. But he was a man of vigorous mind, of deep religious spirit, and great force of character. Feeling himself constrained to proclaim to others the religious convictions that filled his heart, he soon gathered around him a number of followers, of kindred views, and the work gradually extended until several hundreds in the surrounding region looked to him as their leader. These movements naturally excited the opposition of their more worldly neighbors, and especially of the clergy, whose ministrations they neglected. Hahn and his more immediate adherents, under the name of Pietists, still retained their connection with the estab-

lished churches, giving occasional attendance at least on
the ordinances as there administered. Like the earlier
Pietists in Germany, and the first Methodists in England, they hoped to bring about a reformation within
the church itself. They thus escaped in great measure
the persecution which arose against Rapp and his followers, who refused altogether to attend upon the ministrations of the regular clergy, and did not hesitate to
denounce the prevailing worldliness and irreligion.
They were called Separatists; and although demeaning
themselves as quiet, orderly citizens, and paying all
their dues both to church and state, they became objects of general odium, and were denounced to the civil
authorities by the offended clergy. They were per-
secuted with fines and imprisonment, and their appeals
for redress were in vain. After long endurance, and
after having made an ineffectual application to their
own government for permission to form a settlement by
themselves, they determined to emigrate.

In the year 1803, George Rapp, with three or four
others, visited this country in search of a location suitable
for a colony. After examining various localities, they
finally purchased a large tract of land near Zelienople,
in Butler county, Pa. In the autumn of the ensuing
year they were followed by three ship loads of colonists,
most of whom spent the winter in Philadelphia, Baltimore, and elsewhere, while a number of families came
out at once and joined Rapp in the work of building
up a town. These latter passed the winter in the
endurance of great hardships, but by the ensuing
spring had made such progress in their work, that
their waiting brethren could be invited to come and
join them.

Before they left Germany they had embraced some peculiar views of religion and of social economy, to which they were led, as they supposed, by their careful study of the New Testament. They had generally adopted the *millennarian* theory of the personal and pre-millennial advent of Christ, which they regarded as near at hand. They were also disposed to follow the example of the primitive Christians in having all things common, and some of them at least came to this country with the expectation of forming a community on this principle. Thus far, however, each family retained possession of its own property, and had borne for itself the expenses attendant upon emigration.

On the 15th of February, 1805, Rapp and his associates, who had spent the winter in the work of preparation, together with as many of their scattered brethren as could be at that time assembled, proceeded deliberately and solemnly to organize themselves into an association on the principle of community of goods. They threw all their possessions into a common stock; those who had wealth agreeing as cheerfully as those who had nothing, to share henceforth all things in common. They adopted a simple and uniform style of dress, and proceeded to build their family residences as much alike as possible. They assumed the name of the " Harmony Society," and called their town Harmony. They were joined in the spring by about fifty additional families of their brethren, who had tarried in the East and elsewhere, and who were willing to adopt the community principle. Several of those who came over with them chose not to join the association, but became merged in the great American community. The whole number of families ultimately composing the Society was about one hundred and twenty-five.

The writer of the article referred to has but *romanced* in representing that the Harmonists, in adopting their peculiar system, were but dupes in the hands of Rapp, and that he had large property, library, and gallery of paintings, which he surrendered to the Society. Nothing of this is true. On the contrary, some of his followers were more wealthy, and of higher social standing than he, and in point of intelligence and education he was but little superior to many of the respectable tradesmen, mechanics, and agriculturists, who chose him as their leader. He continued to be their acknowledged head, both in religious and secular matters. Indeed, no distinction was made between the civil and religious organization; they all formed one church and one civil community.

There was a *foreman* in each department of business, who was responsible for its proper management, and for the impartial distribution of whatever was necessary for the wants of the individual members. Frederick Rapp, the adopted son of George Rapp, and a young man of fine executive abilities, was appointed the general business agent of the Society for outside matters. These foremen, together with young Rapp, constituted a council or board of assistants to Mr. Rapp, in the management of all their temporal affairs, and in the settlement of any disputes which might arise.

They proceeded as speedily as possible to the clearing off of their lands, and the erection of their church, school house, hotel, mills, barns, manufactories, &c. This was their time of trial. Strangers in a strange

land, ignorant of the language, laws, manners and customs of the country, with scanty resources, and without
friends or established credit, subject to many surmises
and slanderous accusations, besides the internal friction
which naturally attended the first working of their new
system of community life—altogether their faith and
patience were subjected to a severe test. But they
trusted in God, and went forward with patient endurance and true German persistence, until in a few years
all difficulties were surmounted, and prosperity crowned
their toils.

Some two years subsequent to their organization,
under the influence of what they denominate a " fresh
religious revival," they made a further advance toward
what they believed to be a more pure and holy life, by
abjuring matrimony and further conjugal intercourse.
Families continued to dwell together as before, but
henceforth, by mutual agreement, " they that had
wives were as though they had none." Whatever
may be thought of the propriety or impropriety of this
arrangement, it was undoubtedly a purely voluntary
sacrifice, which they were led to make, not from any
pressure of authority on the part of Rapp (as has been
alleged), nor from a desire the more speedily to enrich
themselves by checking the further increase of population, but from strong religious conviction. They believed that such a manner of life was more holy, and
would the better prepare them for the speedy coming
of the Lord. In defense of this view, they plausibly
refer to such passages of Scripture as Matthew 19 : 10,
12; 22 : 30; Revelation 14 : 4, &c. The practice of
celibacy was also only a more full and consistent car-

rying out of their fundamental principle of entire equality in all things, which implied an abstinence on the
part of individuals from every indulgence in which all
alike might not participate.

The same principle was applied to the use of tobacco
The question having arisen as to what gratification
should be allowed to the non-users of the weed, as an
equivalent to that luxury, it was unanimously agreed
that all alike should entirely abstain ; and many a beloved meerschaum was forthwith committed to the
flames.

In all this rigidness of self-denial for conscience sake
and for good fellowship, these people have (as they
supposed) but practiced the duty of cutting off the right
hand and plucking out the right eye, according to our
Saviour's precept ; and certainly their motives cannot
but be admired even by those who do not approve their
practice, or feel called upon to adopt it. It is not to be
supposed, indeed, that this rigid asceticism could be
persistently carried out without occasional lapses.
There were not unfrequent instances of backsliding,
or of withdrawal from the Society on account of these
peculiarities ; but, upon the whole, the great majority
have faithfully and consistently maintained their principles.

The horrid story which the writer of the article in
the *Atlantic* has introduced in regard to the " killing" of
Rapp's son for refusing to be separated from his wife,
is wholly false. It is an old slander which has long
been in circulation, and was published some years ago,
in a grosser form, by some scribbling correspondent of
the Philadelphia *North American.* It was promptly

refuted through the Pittsburgh *Evening Chronicle.* It may be well to reproduce this denial. The editor writes : "As to his son, Rapp never needed to exercise any severity over him. He was a worthy, industrious and exemplary young man, who died in the year 1812, *seven* years after the establishment of the Society in this country." [And I may add, five years after the adoption of celibacy by the community.] "Mr. Baker, the present head of the Society, says that he was at work with him in 1810, elevating grain in the Society's store, when he (young Rapp) strained himself, and injured his breast, which injury finally ended in incurable consumption ; that after his death he was dissected, and a large portion of water was found in his chest, and one lobe of his lungs destroyed." I may add, that I have personally received full corroboration of the above statement from persons who then belonged to the Society, but who withdrew from it, and could have no motive for disguising the facts.

The twaddle of the writer about the silly weakness of the Harmonite women at the sight of a child, is also a gross caricature. All true women (the *strong minded* perhaps excepted) love children. And so do these. But children are every day to be seen among them, being apprenticed orphans, or the children of recent members, or of their hired people, or of lodgers and visitors at their hotel.

I shall only further state, that on the death of George Rapp, in 1847, the Society selected seven elders for the management of their social concerns, and two trustees to conduct their foreign business. These trustees are Messrs. R. L. Baker and Jacob Henrici, the former

of whom also officiates as the spiritual leader and in-
structor of the community, with occasional assistance
from the latter, who is the chief business manager.

The Society has now existed sixty-one years. It
originally consisted of from 600 to 700 souls. In 1832
a great secession took place under a certain self-styled
Count Leon, who drew off one-third of the members
with him. Their number has been further reduced by
withdrawals and deaths, until only about two hundred
and fifty remain. A considerable number also, who
are not members, are employed as apprentices and
hired laborers. The present members are all growing
old. They cheerfully and hopefully await the Lord's
coming, either to call them hence to the upper man-
sions, or to reveal himself in his glory. The organization, in its present form, cannot long be maintained.
What changes may take place in the future, or what
disposition may ultimately be made of the wealth they
have acquired, are matters which they keep within
their own counsels, or perhaps leave to the disposal of
Divine Providence.

It is but a due tribute to this community to add, that
if their industry and economy have been crowned with
the acquisition of wealth, they have not enjoyed it
selfishly. While still retaining their primitive simplicity in dress and style of living, they have always
been accustomed to devise liberal things in the way of
relieving the wants of the poor, and contributing freely
toward all philanthropic enterprises which met their
approbation. They are also intensely patriotic. Though
taking no part in political contests, they bore their full
share in sustaining the Government in its recent terrible

struggle with rebellion.   Far more loyal than thousands
of native American citizens, and most of them being
too old to enter the army in person, they have contributed lavishly for the equipment of volunteers, for
special bounties, for the support of the families of
absent soldiers, for the Christian, Sanitary, and Sub-
sistence Commissions, for the fortification of Pittsburgh,
for the relief of the freedmen, for the support of soldiers' widows, and the education of their orphan children.   Their contributions for these and kindred objects would amount to many thousands of dollars. Such
a people ought not to be slandered.

CHAPTER II.

BIOGRAPHICAL SKETCHES OF GEORGE RAPP AND FREDERICK RAPP.

THE "Economites," as they are popularly called, do not seek publicity, but the public is anxious to know more about them. That an association founded upon principles so diverse from those of our great American community should have been sustained and successfully conducted among us for more than sixty years, is itself a phenomenon which awakens curiosity, and presents a *study* in the science of social economy. From the many questions which have been asked of the writer, he finds that much misapprehension exists as to the principles and practices of the Society. In furnishing such facts as have come into his possession, he wishes but to gratify a desire which generally prevails for authentic information in regard to this people. He appears, however, not as their *advocate*, but only as their historian.

The sketch of the early history of the Society, given in the first chapter, may properly be followed by a more detailed account of the personal history of the founder, George Rapp. He was the son of Adam Rapp, a farmer and vine planter of moderate circumstances, residing in the town of Iptingen, Oberamt Maulbronn, kingdom of Würtemberg. George Rapp was born in said town on the 28th of October, 1757. He was brought up as usual among his class of people, enjoying the benefits of a common school education, where seldom more than reading, writing, arithmetic and geography were taught.

After his school years, he assisted his father on the farm in summer, and worked a hand-loom in winter. In the year 1783 he married a farmer's daughter, Christina Benzinger, who bore him a son, John, the father of Gertrude (who is still a member of the Harmony Society), and a daughter, Rosina. The circumstances of John's death (about which the Society has been so foully slandered) were given in our former chapter. He died of consumption in 1812. Rosina died of old age in 1849. George Rapp had also one brother and two sisters, who died many years ago. Frederick Rapp, whose name is more generally known, was only an adopted son, and not a kinsman. He was George Rapp's most efficient helper in founding and subsequently managing the affairs of the Society. A further notice of him will be given below.

George Rapp was fond of reading and conversation, and having an active and inquiring mind, he soon added largely, by his own study of books and men, to his stores of knowledge acquired at school. Being naturally of a religious turn, he studied the Bible closely, especially the New Testament, and became convinced that the so-called Christians generally, so far as he could learn, "did not at all live up to the duties and practices required by the doctrine of Christ and his apostles." At about thirty years of age, not finding the necessary spiritual nourishment in the established church to which he belonged, he began to speak in his own house, to a small number of friends, his sentiments on religion, once or twice every Sunday. The number of his hearers increased, and gradually people from other towns, ten or twelve miles distant, came to his meetings, so that by the time when an emigration to America was spoken of, his adherents numbered some three hundred families.

The clergy set themselves in opposition to Rapp's religious labors. They instigated the civil authorities against him and his followers, and tried their best to prevent their meetings. This was hard to do, because Mr. Rapp advised his people to be obedient to the laws, and to the punctual payment of all taxes to church and state, so that the sole ground of accusation against him and his party was their separation from the church, and their holding of private religious meetings. Police officers were sent to examine, and to enroll all persons present at these assemblages, not only in the town where Rapp resided and preached, but also in other towns where his adherents also held similar meetings. On Mondays they would be summoned to appear before the magistrates, and were fined for attendance upon these conventicles. Those who were too poor to pay were imprisoned. These persecutions were carried so far at last, that a petition was addressed to the king, asking for a decree of banishment against Rapp and his followers. The king inquired, " Who are these people ? Are they good citizens ? Do they pay their taxes ? " &c. And being informed that they were always among the first to pay all their dues both to the church and state, and that they were good and orderly citizens, he tore the petition to pieces and said, " *Then let them believe as they please.*"

Notwithstanding the refusal of the king to molest Rapp or his followers, the clergy still continued their opposition, by stirring up the mayors and burgesses of the towns against them, so that the fines and imprisonments and other annoyances were kept up for several years, until at length they felt themselves called of the Lord to leave their native land. They were a devout people, and sought only to know and to do the will of God. Michael Hahn and his followers, who entertained similar views, in other respects, chose not to separate themselves entirely from fellowship with the established Lutheran Church, but preferred to yield somewhat to the demands of the state, and to prosecute the work of reformation, as best they might, by remaining at home. Rapp and his party were made of sterner stuff, and were stigmatized as *separatists*. They became more open and violent in their denunciation of the prevailing vices and religious corruptions. The alienation between them and their neighbors thus naturally increased, and their position became more unpleasant. Nor would it be strange in the circumstances, that something of a spirit of religious fanaticism should be developed, and that Rapp should be impressed with a belief that he had a special divine mission to the work to which he was thus providentially called.

At length, in 1803, at the request of his brethren, he set forth, accompanied by his son John and two or three friends, to visit America. Leaving his family and the interests of his as yet unorganized society of followers, under the supervision of his adopted son Frederick, Rapp and his companions embarked at Amsterdam, and after a safe voyage arrived at Baltimore, where they found friends who received them with much kindness, as they did Rapp's people afterward.

They spent some time in exploring parts of Maryland and Pennsylvania, and as far west in Ohio as the valley of the Tuscarawas river. Believing it too great a risk to take one hundred or more families so far into the backwoods, as that part of Ohio then was, they preferred to settle in a more inhabited region, and finally selected a desirable location about twenty-five miles north of Pittsburgh, in Butler county, Pennsylvania. They purchased about five thousand acres of unimproved land from Dr. Detmar Basse, a wealthy German, who had settled there some years before. These lands are located in the beautiful valley of the Connoquenessing, near to where Zelienople now stands.

As soon as Rapp's people in Germany could be notified of the purchase, they were ready to follow, all the necessary arrangements for the voyage having been previously made through the efficient agency of Frederick Rapp. Early in the spring of 1804, the ship *Aurora* sailed from Amsterdam with three hundred souls, and landed in Baltimore, July 4th, of the same year. The ship *Atlantic* landed a similar number at Philadelphia, about six weeks later. The ship *Margaretta* brought the remainder of the people, but most of those who came in this vessel were led, from various causes, to make a settlement in Lycoming county, Pennsylvania, under the direction of a Mr. Haller, who had been one

of Mr. Rapp's companions in the mission of explora-
tion.

Rapp met his friends who came over in the first
ship, on their arrival in Baltimore, and saw that they
were distributed in small parties in different parts of
the country, where they might sojourn until habitations could be prepared for them at Harmony, by himself and the party of workmen detailed for that purpose.   Having passed a winter of great hardship in the
work of building and preparing, he was ready by the
ensuing February (1805) to receive as many of his
waiting people as could then be assembled from their
various places of sojourn.   At this time the first formal organization of the Society on the principle of
community of goods took place, as narrated in our former chapter.

To give Rapp's subsequent personal history would
be to give the history of the Society in detail for more
than forty years.   He was its civil and religious head,
its prophet, priest, and king.   He dictated all its rules
and regulations, and was the supreme arbiter in all
questions that arose.   His word was law.   It was
enough to know that " Father Rapp says it," to
satisfy all the community on any subject whatever. All
this power, however, was administered, not selfishly or
tyrannically, but in a truly patriarchal spirit, and with
a single eye to the temporal and spiritual welfare of
his people, who loved and reverenced him as a father,
and never thought of questioning his right to all the
authority which he claimed.   It is not to be wondered
at that he became impatient of contradiction or opposition, and had a reputation for harshness and severity

among outsiders and excommunicated members. He did not hesitate to fulminate spiritual thunders against bold transgressors, whom he regarded as offending not only against the accepted rules of the Society, but also against the authority of God, which was claimed as sanctioning the principles on which the Society was founded. But he was as *fatherly* in his kindness as he was in his severity toward his people, whom he regarded as his children. He sympathized with them in their trials, consoled them in their perplexities, patiently instructed them in the truths of religion, and sought in every way to make them all happy. While all were expected to be busy, none were allowed to be burdened with work. Ample time was afforded for rest and recreation. Being fond of music, as all Germans are, he encouraged the cultivation of both vocal and instrumental music among all the members, and especially the young people. Their evening leisure was enlivened with the strains which a well trained band discoursed, and their religious services were always accompanied with the finest singing by the whole congregation, led by instruments and a skillful choir. He divided the whole community into Classes— the old men and the old women, the young men and the young women, and the more youthful of both sexes, each separately forming a class, which met once or twice a week for social intercourse and mutual improvement. The members of these classes were taught to regard each other as brothers and sisters, and to watch fraternally over each other's conduct and deportment, and were accustomed, as far as possible, to settle among themselves all little difficulties that might arise. Mr.

Rapp met with these several classes himself as often as possible, for religious conference or more free social conversation.

Thus he dwelt, year after year, among his own peo ple, more and more beloved and reverenced by them as they grew old together. He and his immediate family fared no better than the rest of the community in the matter of dress or style of living, except that for the honor of the Society he was expected to live in a larger and better house, where friends and guests might re- ceive hospitality, and on special occasions to appear in a state dress made of their own finest silk fabrics. But he never accumulated any private property for himself or his family. Everything belonged to the Society.

Thus, through all the vicissitudes of the Society's history (which I reserve for future notice), George Rapp continued his wise and benign administration, down to his ninetieth year, still retaining his faculties, voice, energy, and physical powers in such vigor, that he was able, until within a few days before his death, to preach two sermons every Sabbath, and one on Wed- nesday evening, and to be present at five class meetings during the week.

He had lived so long among them, and with so little apparent waning of his powers, that some of his people were weak enough to believe that "Father Rapp would never die," or at least that he would abide until the Lord's coming. There were but three Sabbaths that he failed to appear as usual in the pulpit, and even on the last of these he preached to his people with his wonted energy and power of voice, from the window of the room where he was confined by physical weakness. His limbs only refused to perform their office. But the machinery of life was worn out, and before another Sabbath, after bidding farewell in person to all his sorrowing people, as they came one by one to his bedside, he peaceably expired, in full confidence of meeting the Lord in the better world. He died on the 7th of August, 1847, lacking a few weeks of being ninety years of age.

He was a remarkable man, and had performed a remarkable work. Had he been a propagandist, and lived in a different age and country, he might have been known as the founder of a new sect or nation. But he had no other thought than the welfare of the small body of people who had followed him from Germany, for the purpose of serving God in their own way. He left his impress on the Society, which still exists much as he left it, only with diminished numbers.

After the simple funeral was over, his body having been deposited in the orchard, where his grave is undistinguished by any mark from those of his brethren who sleep around him, the Society all assembled in the church to consider what was to be done. They were like a family of children bereaved of its head. They felt that they had no one who could fill Father Rapp's place, but they still approved of the principles upon which he had founded and governed the Society, and they determined to carry them out. With great unanimity, they elected from among themselves a board of nine elders, upon whom were devolved the powers heretofore exercised by Rapp himself, with the advice and assistance of the foremen and business agents of the Society. Two of these elders, R. L. Baker and J. Henrici, were designated as Trustees, and became the executive officers as well as the religious guides of the community. It was a remarkable evidence of the confidence which Mr. Rapp's administration had inspired, that not an individual member called for any report or statement as to the pecuniary affairs of the Society. They took it for granted that all was right. And that this confidence was not misplaced, was made apparent a few years afterward, in the progress of certain trials instituted against the Society by seceding members. The most protracted and searching investigations by the courts, with such men as Charles Shaler and Edwin M. Stanton as the lawyers for the prosecution, failed to discover any maladministration, or misappropriation of funds on the part of Rapp or his associates.

A brief notice of Frederick Rapp may close this chapter. His proper name was Frederick Reichert; he was born in Germany, April 12th, 1775. He was a stone cutter and architect by trade; he had received a good education, of such a grade as the ordinary public schools of the country afforded. His travels in the prosecution of his business brought him into the neighborhood where George Rapp resided, and he soon made his acquaintance, and became an attendant upon his meetings. He found the teachings of Rapp to meet his own sense of religious want, and to correspond with the growing convictions which his own mind had been cherishing. He was like many others who declared that "of all the preachers whom they had heard, there was none whose words had power to touch their hearts

like those of Mr. Rapp." Frederick soon became a
devoted adherent, and a member of Rapp's family.
And when the great measure of emigration was at
length resolved upon, his fine executive abilities found
scope in conducting the necessary arrangements. As
stated above, when George Rapp came to America,
Frederick was left in charge of his family and of the
religious work which he had inaugurated.

He enrolled the names of those who proposed to
emigrate, secured from their wealthier brethren the
necessary aid for those who were not able to meet the
expenses of the voyage, corresponded with the ship
owners at Amsterdam, and, in short, did whatever was
necessary to forward the great enterprise which they
had in view. After dispatching the first ship with its
instalment of colonists, he himself remained until all
the rest were ready, and then came over with them in
one of the ships which landed at Philadelphia.

So faithfully and efficiently had he discharged his
various trusts, that by the unanimous consent of the
Society at its organization, he was associated with
George Rapp in the management of its affairs. It was
also by the desire of Mr. Rapp himself and of the
Society, that Frederick dropped the name of Reichert,
and became recognized as the adopted son of George
Rapp. As the spiritual functions and the home management were sufficient to occupy all the time of George
Rapp, Frederick was intrusted with the affairs of the
exterior, for which his business capacity so well fitted
him. He conducted all negotiations in the way of
purchase and sale with those outside of the Society,
did the necessary traveling to Pittsburgh, Philadelphia,

&c., and conducted any outside litigation which might occasionally arise. He carried on in his own name all the external business of the Society, taking to himself the titles of real estate, and holding it in his own name, though under a solemn contract, signed and sealed, in which he declares that all the property, personal, real and mixed, which then was or should afterward be in his possession, or held in his name, should be the sole and absolute property of the Society, and not of himself.

He continued to serve the Society in this capacity, with great success, and to the acceptance of all, down to the year of his death. In the latter part of the year 1833 he had somehow taken a cold, which was increased by the eagerness with which he exposed himself on the famous night of the "shooting stars," a phenomenon on which he gazed with intense interest. He soon became dropsical and otherwise permanently diseased, and died in the following June, 1834, while the prayers of the whole assembled Society were ascending for the continuance of his life. One who sat with him the last night of his life, cherishes a most impressive remembrance of his pious and instructive conversation during that solemn night.

Frederick Rapp was accustomed to officiate as preacher in case of the absence or illness of George Rapp. He was a man of considerable literary culture, and poetic ability, several of the hymns in the Society's collection being composed by him. He was well known and highly esteemed among a large circle of business acquaintances ; and being a well bred gentleman and good musician, as well as an amateur in works of art, he was a welcome visitor in many a family circle, whose hospitalities he was always glad to reciprocate as he had opportunity.

After the death of Frederick, it became necessary that another business agent should be appointed in his place ; and on the 5th of July, 1834, Mr. George Rapp, although he had so long been the general head of the whole Society, was now, for the first time, formally designated to this secular office, in a document signed by all the members.   In this document, which is in the nature of a mutual contract, George Rapp solemnly disclaims all personal interest in the property of the Society, other than that of an individual member.   Being himself still occupied chiefly with his spiritual and other home functions, he appointed as sub-agents, R. L. Baker and J. Henrici, who attended to those details of outside business which had belonged to Frederick Rapp during his life.

CHAPTER III.

THEIR HISTORY AT OLD HARMONY.

*REASONS FOR ADOPTING THE COMMUNITY SYSTEM, AND
CELIBACY —TRIALS AND TRIUMPHS.*

THE former chapters have contained only the most brief notice of the history of the Society subsequent to its first organization.   Some further details may be of interest.   It will be remembered that the followers of Rapp came from Germany, still retaining their personal property and former domestic relations, and each family at its own expense.   They came, however, most of them at least, with the intention of adopting the community system, but with no definite purpose, as yet, with reference to the abandonment of marriage and conjugal intercourse, although this latter subject had been somewhat discussed among them.

On their assembling at Harmony, some were moderately wealthy, while others had nothing left after defraying the expenses of their immigration.   They were thus in the condition of the primitive Christians at Jerusalem, of whom some were rich and some poor, many of the latter being destitute, by having come from a distance to the great feast of the Passover, without bringing with them the funds necessary for their expenses during the unexpected delay occasioned by their conversion to Christianity. Thus, in that instance, it became a matter of the most obvious Christian obligation, that those resident in Jerusalem, or the vicinity, who were possessors of lands or houses, should sell them and lay down the proceeds at the apostles' feet, so that distribution should be made to every man according as he had need. The wants of the poorer brethren and of those who were strangers, were thus supplied, and, for the time being at least, they "had all things common." Rapp and his people, however, so understood the Scriptures, that they felt bound not only to imitate this example in their present emergency, but to adopt it as a permanent and fundamental principle in their organization. They regarded the gospel as requiring the abnegation of all our selfish feelings, and looked upon the pursuit of personal gain—the "love of money"—as "the root of all evil," inconsistent alike with that supreme love to God and that spirit of true equality and brotherhood, which are of the very essence of religion. Their expectation also of the Lord's probable speedy coming rendered them the more indifferent to the possession of worldly goods. It was under the influence of such motives that most of those who joined Rapp at Harmony were ready, with one accord, of their own free will, and without undue pressure of authority from him, to enter into the mutual covenant which they solemnly adopted on the 15th of February, 1805. It may, however, be mentioned as among their early trials, that a few of those who had come over as Rapp's followers were not disposed to enter into this organization, but used their liberty in retaining their personal property and merging themselves with the outside world. About ten families, including some of the most wealthy among them, became dissatisfied with the socialistic views of the majority, and withdrew both their aid and their funds, to the great grief of their brethren, and to the great pecuniary loss of the Society. In this connection may also be mentioned another serious difficulty which arose soon after their organization.

Their town of Harmony was located within one mile of the older village of Zelienople, which Dr. Basse had founded. A competition arose between these two places as to which should have the post-office, and the post road which was being laid out between Pittsburgh and Lake Erie. It was reported to the disadvantage of the Harmonists that they were at variance among themselves, that they could not pay for their lands, that the Society was likely to be soon broken up and their town abandoned, and that the road and post-office would not be needed there. And, although they gained both the road and post-office, and paid for their lands sooner than their obligations required, yet the evil report had gone abroad to the injury of their credit. When Frederick Rapp next visited Pittsburgh, and called at a house with which he had before dealt, he was refused even a short credit on the articles which he wished to purchase. On inquiry as to the cause, he was answered that common report said that the Society was on the eve of breaking up.

So long as they had to buy all their provisions and supplies, their fare was coarse and scant, and they knew sometimes what it was to feel the gnawings of

hunger. Their work of grubbing and clearing off
land was a hard toil to which they had not been accustomed. In these circumstances, weak and disaffected
members were ready to communicate to outsiders all
the difficulties, smaller or greater, which occurred in
the Society, and these again were further reported
abroad with exaggeration, so that the public eye was
continually fixed with jealousy and distrust on this
strange community. Thus sorely were they tried
during the first year or two after their settlement.

These trials, however, were only what the more
thoughtful among them had anticipated, and they were
prepared to meet them. Before they left Germany,
some of them were often heard to say, in the midst of
their persecutions, that "if they could only find a land
where religious toleration was enjoyed, they would wish
to be there, even though they might have for a while
to live upon roots." They were never reduced quite to
this extremity, but their trials were sufficiently severe
to test the faith of the most earnest and devout, and
they regard them since as providential visitations, designed to inure them to that life of self-denial and crucifixion of the flesh which their whole system involves.

The terms of the agreement mutually entered into
between " George Rapp and his associates" on the one
part, and the other members of the Society on the
other part, were in substance as follows, viz.: 1. Those
of the latter part, for themselves and their heirs and
descendants, agree to deliver up all their estates and
property whatever, in cash, lands, chattels, &c., as a
free gift or donation, for the benefit and use of the
community, and to be at the disposal of the superin-

tendents, as though they had never possessed it.
2. They also pledged themselves to submit to the laws
and regulations of the community ; to show a ready
obedience to the superintendents; to give the labor of
their hands for the good of the community, and to hold
their children and families to do the same. 3. In case
any, contrary to their present expectation, should at
any future time desire to withdraw from the Society,
from whatever cause, they were never to demand any
remuneration for labor or services rendered by themselves or their children.

George Rapp and his associates, on the other hand,
agree on their part, 1. To adopt the other contracting
parties as members of the community, whereby each of
them obtains the privilege of being present at each
religious meeting, and they and their children and
families are to receive such instruction in church and
school as was needful and requisite for their temporal
welfare and eternal felicity. 2. Rapp and his associates promise to supply the members with all the
necessaries of life, not only during their days of health
and strength, but during sickness, old age, or incapac-
ity to labor; and to the widows and orphans of any
member, the same rights and maintenance are to be
afforded as long as they shall live or remain members
of the community. 3. In case of the withdrawal of
any member or members of the community for whatever cause, George Rapp and his associates engage to
refund to him or them the value of their property
originally brought into the Society, without interest;
and if they had brought nothing in, they should receive a donation in money according to their conduct

during membership, &c.   [This last provision in regard to *refunding* was abrogated in 1836, as will be hereafter explained.   See Appendix D, and Chapter VII.] Persons who subsequently joined the Society, were received on the same conditions, after one year of satisfactory probation, and on subscribing to the above articles.

The association being thus fully organized, and the few thousands of which their aggregate fund consisted having been invested in payment for their lands, and for articles of immediate necessity, all hands in this busy hive go diligently to work in clearing out their lands, cultivating the soil, pursuing trades, and erecting the necessary buildings.   During the first year, one hundred and fifty acres of ground were cleared, from forty to fifty log houses were erected, besides a house of worship, a grist mill, large barn, shops, &c.   Next year, they clear four hundred acres more of land, and erect a saw mill, tannery, distillery, brick store house, &c., and plant a vineyard of four acres.   They raise grain enough for themselves, and have six hundred bushels to sell, besides three thousand gallons of whiskey.   This latter manufacture is one in which they have always excelled, though much more to their own pecuniary profit than to their credit as a religious and comparatively temperate community, or to the welfare of the surrounding people and neighborhood.

They engaged to some extent also in the culture of the vine, to which most of them had been accustomed in Germany.   In 1809 they produced six thousand bushels of Indian corn, four thousand five hundred of wheat, four thousand five hundred of rye, five thousand of oats, ten thousand of potatoes, four thousand pounds of flax and hemp, and fifty gallons of sweet oil made from the poppy. During this year also they made their first piece of woolen cloth from yarn spun by hand, which was regarded as a great step toward independence. In 1810 they erected a woolen factory for the manufacture of broadcloth from the wool of the Merino sheep, which they were among the first to introduce into this country, and which became one of the great sources of their growing wealth.* Not to speak in detail of their progress from year to year in agricultural, mechanical and commercial prosperity, we find that in 1810, five years after their organization, they consisted of one hundred and forty families, amounting in the whole to seven hundred or eight hundred persons; that they have two thousand acres of land under cultivation ; that they have a large stock of the finest sheep and cattle, and that in every department of labor they have a large surplus for sale after supplying all their own wants. They have their own tradesmen of all the necessary varieties; carpenters, blacksmiths, wagon makers, coopers, shoe makers, hatters, tailors, masons, wheelwrights, saddlers, &c., &c., who serve not only their own community, but also the surrounding country, all their work being most honestly and faithfully done.

A writer who visited them about this time, has given the following testimony concerning them: "We are

---

*.In regard to the introduction of these sheep, a written memorandum thus states : " An Eastern man named Hopkins, had sent from New York one hundred Merino ewes into our neighborhood for sale. But the people generally were not prepared to pay one hundred and twenty-five or one hundred and fifty dollars for one sheep, and they

struck with surprise and admiration at the astonishing
progress in improvements and the establishment of
manufactories which this little republic has made in
the period of five years.   They have indeed made the
' wilderness to blossom as the rose.'   They have done
more essential good for this country in the short period
of five years, than the same number of families scattered about the country have done in fifty.   And this
arises from their unity and brotherly love, added to
their uniform and persevering industry.   They know
no mercenary view, no self interest, except that which
adds to the interest and happiness of the whole community.   All are equally industrious, for an idler has
no companion.   If any should fall into bad practices of
idleness or intoxication, he is kindly admonished by
the head of the family, backed by the countenance and
wishes of all the rest; but if he is found incorrigible,
he is excluded from the Society; so that there is no
opening for the practice of vice and immorality.   All attend the place of worship twice on each Sabbath, and
give serious audience to the words of their venerable
father and preacher, George Rapp, who, from his manner, appears devoted both to the spiritual and temporal
interests of his flock.   They have also sermon twice
every week.   The children are kept at school from six
to fourteen, and then are put to such trades as they
may choose.   Sometimes nearly the whole force of the
Society, male and female, is put to one object, such as

would have been driven back, had we not bought them at one hundred
dollars a head. We now increased our flock, introduced Merino sheep
into the neighborhood, paid two dollars a pound for unwashed Merino
wool, and improved the manufacture of broadcloth, which sold for
twelve dollars per yard in the time of the embargo."

pulling flax, reaping, hoeing corn, &c., so that the labor of a hundred acre field is accomplished in a day or two. All in fact seems to go on like clock-work, and all seem contented and happy."

This picture is doubtless in the main correct, though sufficiently flattering. Its substantial truthfulness could be verified by a visit to the community at any subsequent period, down to the present time. There is friction no doubt in the machinery. Human nature is not a sort of material to work smoothly, even in the most favorable circumstances. But in this Society the oil of brotherly love, and Christian charity, and meek contentment, is so well applied, that the creaking of the machinery is seldom heard even by one standing near at hand.

The subject of celibacy we noticed somewhat in our first chapter. It is here introduced again, as one of the most noticeable events in the history of the Society during their residence at Old Harmony. It may also be stated, more fully, that marriage was not discountenanced during the first two years of the Society's existence. During that period a number of marriages took place, solemnized by Rapp himself; among others was that of his own son John (father of Gertrude), who married therefore with his father's full approbation.

There was, however, in the views of the Society some tendency to asceticism, and the question whether there was not a holier state than that of matrimony was agitated among them. In 1807, a much deeper religious feeling than usual pervaded the Society. They call it a " fresh revival of religion," such as had given rise to their first movement in Germany. Deep

convictions of sin were experienced, and a general
sense of worldliness and backsliding. They acknowledged to each other their consciousness of want of con-
formity to the spirit of primitive Christianity, which
they aimed to restore. Among other things, they fixed
upon the indulgences of the married state, as generally
practiced, as not being consistent with that purity of
heart and isolation from the world which they desired
to cultivate. Such, at least, is their own account of
the matter. Protestant Christians generally will say,
that a more intelligent and scriptural view of the whole
subject would have led to very different conclusions.
But Mr. Rapp encouraged and strongly advocated the
growing ascetic spirit. Such passages of Scripture as
seem to favor the practice of celibacy, were expounded
and urged as applicable to all periods of the church, as
well as to the peculiar circumstances of the primitive
Christians. Some of these passages were referred to
in a former articles. They are such as Matt. 19:10–12
and 22:30; 1 Cor. 7:7, 8, and 25–27, 29; 1 Thess.
4:3–5; Rev. 14:4. He did not condemn matrimony
as being unlawful in those who had not within themselves a *vocation* to what he regarded as a holier state.
But in view, especially, of the expected near approach
of the Messiah's second advent, and of that " first resurrection" in which " they neither marry nor are given
in marriage," &c., and in order that they might be numbered among the " hundred and forty-four thousand"
who should " stand with the Lamb on Mount Zion,"
and "who were such as were not defiled with women,
but were virgins," he urged his people to this great
work of purification and preparation.

As an evidence of his sincerity, he himself set an example by practicing what he preached, as did also his son John (not by force and violence, as the slander has it, but of his own free will). These, with other leaders, and at length the members generally who were married, agreed to abstain from further conjugal intercourse. No more marriages were solemnized, and it became established as a law of the Society that marriage was incompatible with membership. Thus this tenderest of earthly bonds was virtually sundered among them. Many of the members being yet young, the trial, as may well be imagined, was a very severe one, too much so indeed for the faith and fortitude of some. Hence the lapses, back-slidings and withdrawals to which we alluded before.

It may be doubted also whether this trial was alleviated by the fact stated by one of their number, that " husbands and wives were not required to live in different houses, but occupied, as before, the same dwelling with their family, treating each other as brother and sister in Christ, and remembering the precept of the Apostle, ' This, I say, brethren, the time is short; it remaineth that both they that have wives be as though they had none,' " &c. He adds, that " it was easier to bear, because it became general through the whole community, and all bore their share alike." Another, writing in 1862, says : "Convinced of the truth and holiness of our purpose, we voluntarily and unanimously adopted celibacy, altogether from religious motives, in order to withdraw our love entirely from the lusts of the flesh, which, with the help of God, and much prayer and spiritual warfare, we have succeeded well in doing now for fifty years."

No children have been born in the community for many years, and the general consistency of their practice with their principles on this subject, affords a remarkable example of steadfastness in resistance to the flesh.

It may not be amiss here to correct another of the formerly current slanders, to which the greater notoriety has been given by its introduction into the poems of Lord Byron, where he says,

"When Rapp the Harmonist embargoed marriage," &c.

It is, that while marriage is not prohibited, it is so restricted " as to prevent more than a certain quantum of births in a certain number (seven) of years," &c.

To any one well acquainted with the history of the Society, it is needless to say, that *there never has been any ground whatever for such a statement.* Their reasons for the adoption of celibacy must have entirely prohibited any such usage.

It is one of the multitude of gross slanders which have been put in circulation by the enemies of the Society, and credited by those who cannot comprehend how such rigid self-denial should be practiced for conscience sake.

CHAPTER IV.

REMOVAL TO THE WABASH, AND FINAL SET-
TLEMENT AT ECONOMY.

*THEY SETTLE IN POSEY COUNTY, INDIANA—ENLARGED
OPERATIONS, AND INCREASE OF NUMBERS—SELL OUT
TO ROBERT OWEN, AND RETURN TO PENNSYLVANIA—
TOWN OF ECONOMY BUILT—THEY ENGAGE IN THE SILK
BUSINESS— ÆSTHETIC CULTURE—DUKE OF SAXE WEI-
MAR'S VISIT—ARCADIA LOSES ITS ROMANCE— OTHER
CHANGES—WINE MAKING.*

HAVING in the previous chapters given the early
and most eventful portion of the history of the
Harmony Association, the subsequent period
may be passed over more cursorily. They continued
to grow and prosper in their original location, as heretofore described, until the year 1814, when they determined to seek a new home. Among their reasons for
desiring a change, was the disadvantage of being twelve
miles from navigation, together with the unfitness of
the soil and climate for the most successful cultivation
of the grape and other fruits, to which they desired to
give special attention. Accordingly they sent a depu-
tation to the West, for the purpose of searching out and
purchasing a more desirable place for their settlement.
They finally selected a large and most inviting body of
lands in the valley of the Wabash, mostly in Posey
county, Indiana, where they purchased some thirty
thousand acres, consisting chiefly of unimproved Gov-

ernment land, along with several improved tracts bought from individuals.

Here they found good lands, good mill seats, a navigable river, and a climate suitable for wine. In the middle of June, 1814, about one hundred persons started down the Ohio river in flat boats, and made the necessary preparations for the reception of their brethren, who followed in detached companies, some in the fall of 1814, and the remainder in the spring of 1815 descending the river in keel and flat boats, as the mode of travel then was.

They had in the meantime disposed of their property in Pennsylvania, at a great sacrifice ; about six thousand acres of land, with all the factories, mills, and other buildings, of the town of Old Harmony, having been sold for one hundred thousand dollars.

They soon built up a new town on the same general plan with the one they had left, with such improvements in the details as their experience suggested. They gave it the name of Harmony, as before.*   Here they greatly enlarged their operations in every department of business, cultivating more land, and raising more stock, erecting larger mills and more extensive manufactories of woolen and cotton goods, and, especially, extending their vineyards and the production of wine. They found the soil and climate here very congenial for this favorite employment. They carried on also a large commerce with the surrounding country, to which they became the great business centre, and they extended their trade even to New Orleans. Besides a large and well stocked store in their

* It was afterward named New Harmony by Robert Owen.

own town, they ultimately established branches in Vin-
cennes, and Shawneetown, furnishing to a large section
of country not only their own productions, but a general supply of dry goods, hardware, agricultural imple-
ments, &c. Their wealth and prosperity, of course,
rapidly increased. They were brought extensively into
contact with the outside world. Their fame became
known, and considerable additions were made to their
number by the admission of new members from Germany, and from German settlers in this country. In
the fall of 1817, an addition of one hundred and thirty
souls was received at one time, consisting of immi-
grants from Würtemberg, many of them being relatives
or acquaintances of the original members. They left
Germany in the same faith, and for the same reasons
which had led to Rapp's emigration, and it is a fact
worthy of notice, that the emigration of a colony to
Russian Tartary, and another to Zoar, Ohio, which are
referred to in the Introduction and in Appendix B,
took place in the same year; showing that the same
influences still continued to operate extensively in that
country.

In the following year (1818), by the advice of Mr.
Rapp, and for the purpose of promoting the greater harmony and equality between the original members and
those more recently added, the book containing the list
of contributions made by any of the members to the
common stock of property owned by the Society, was
burnt. They were exhorted, at the same time, not to
set their hearts upon their worldly possessions, but to
forget those things, and be " as though they possessed
not." This was the palmy period of the Society, as to

numbers and outward prosperity. Their whole number ultimately was not much less than one thousand.

Their subsequent history while on the Wabash, does not furnish any incident of very special interest. They found the surrounding population to be composed pretty largely of settlers from the Southern States, and these not of the best character. Many of them were ignorant, vicious, and turbulent; and sometimes unpleasant collisions occurred between them and the peacefully disposed Harmonists. The country, also, was found to be unhealthy, fevers, agues, &c., prevailing. These circumstances induced them to think of returning to Pennsylvania.

They employed a certain Richard Flower, an Englishman, and a prominent member of an English settlement in their vicinity, at Albion, Illinois, to negotiate for a sale of their lands and other real estate, offering him five thousand dollars to find them a purchaser. Flower went to England for this purpose, and hearing of Robert Owen's community at New Lanark, Scotland, he sought him out, and succeeded in selling to him the town of New Harmony, with all its houses, mills, factories, &c., and twenty thousand acres of land, for one hundred and fifty thousand dollars. This was an immense sacrifice, but they were determined to leave the country, and they submitted to the loss. Having, in the meantime, made a purchase of their present lands in Beaver county, Pennsylvania, on the Ohio river, about eighteen miles from Pittsburgh, they built a steamboat, and removed in detachments to their new and final place of settlement. This was in 1825. Thus they lived ten years at Old Harmony, in Butler county,

Pennsylvania, and ten years at New Harmony, on the Wabash. In both these removals, the whole Society clung together. Some had a reluctance to making these changes, but when the option was given them of remaining behind, with a certain provision made for their wants, or of removing with the rest, they all determined to follow Father Rapp and their brethren.

Their new town, to which they gave the name of Economy, was built on the north side of the Ohio river, on one of the most beautiful sites to be found anywhere in the country. It is in the midst of an elevated plateau, which extends some four miles up and down the Ohio, and slopes gently back to the picturesque hills which skirt it at the distance of nearly a mile from the river. The streets are sixty feet wide, and are at right angles with each other, forming several squares of about two acres and three-quarters each, on the corners of which, and mid-way on the intervening sides, the houses are erected, the enclosed grounds affording ample space for the gardens of the several families. The houses are of frame or brick, two stories high, and of a unique style of *economic* architecture, having but one door each, which is entered through a yard from the side. Their church, hotel, barns, mills, manufactories, &c., were erected as rapidly as possible after their arrival, and on improved plans, practical utility rather than superfluous ornament being consulted. The whole machinery of the Society's operations was soon in vigorous motion as before. The ague-shaken members recovered their lost health. The surrounding population was friendly, and pleasant business and social relations were formed with the neighbors, which have ever since been maintained.

Extensive orchards and vineyards were planted, and soon added their products to the wealth derived from broad fields of grain, large flocks and herds, and busy manufacturing establishments. Labor-saving machinery was introduced. Steam power was then and is still employed wherever it is available. Not only their woolen and cotton factories, their flouring mill, and saw mill, &c., were driven by steam, but they still thresh and clean their grain by steam, grind and press their apples and grapes by steam, and wash and wring their clothes by steam. Their laundry establishment has always been an object of interest, especially to lady visitors. The town is amply supplied with water through wells, hydrants, and watering troughs, at convenient points. A large reservoir receives the water of a stream that flows from the hills, and when this source of supply becomes deficient, the ever serviceable steam engine pumps water from a deep river-well.

In former years they employed the steamboat navigation of the Ohio river as their chief channel of trade and travel; but in later years they enjoy the advantage of the Pittsburgh, Ft. Wayne & Chicago, and the Pittsburgh & Cleveland rail roads, whose trains are passing every hour along the bluff in front of the town. They have also a telegraph office.

Soon after their settlement at Economy, a few silk worms were sent to Mr. Rapp from a friend in the East, with instructions as to the various processes of silk culture. It was a new business to them, but they engaged in it with zeal, as a source of probable profit, and as affording easy employment to the women and children and aged persons among them. They planted an orchard of Italian mulberry and of morus multicaulis, and adorned their streets with shade trees of the same. They soon produced large quantities of raw silk, and looms became necessary for weaving. They employed the services successively, of an Englishman, a Frenchman, and a Switzer, to instruct and assist their own mechanics in the erecting of looms, and the weaving of ribbons, vestings, satins, velvets, &c., in which they soon attained a high degree of skill. The business was successfully continued for a few years, but through want of suitable patronage from the Government, in the way of protection against foreign competition, it was found to be unprofitable, and was at length abandoned by them, as it was also at most other places where it had been introduced.

These Harmonists were not mere boors or dull utilitarians, as they have been falsely represented. It is true that, in addition to their three daily meals, they were accustomed, as they still are, to take a slight lunch in the middle of the forenoon and afternoon (the latter being called " vespers"), consisting of a slice of bread and a mug of wine, beer, or cider; and perhaps some of them may have had these creature-comforts at hand even during the night; but still they did not live merely to eat and drink. They were fond of music, and gave much attention to its cultivation, as already noticed. In their earlier days, also, they were not regardless of works of taste and ornament. The Rapps showed their wisdom in this respect. Frederick especially, being a man of fine æsthetic culture in poetry, music, painting, sculpture, and articles of *virtu*, endeavored to infuse his own spirit into the people.

For this purpose, among things, he procured from New York and Philadelphia, at an expense of several thousand dollars, an extensive museum of curiosities, consisting of rare minerals, fine paintings, collections of birds, insects, shells, &c., besides Indian antiquities, and many other things new and strange. Among the early recollections of the writer, is the expansion of his organ of wonder by the marvels which he saw in this museum. Equally vivid is his recollection of his boyish delight on seeing for the first time a park of deer at Economy. Also, of his losing himself in the mazes of the mysterious labyrinth, composed of a curiously constructed hedge which then grew around and almost concealed from view the round-house that still stands on the outskirts of the village. And then again was West's great picture of " Christ Healing the Sick," which still adorns the parlor of the Rapp House, conspicuous among other fine pictures there to be seen. But most frequented then, as ever since, was " Rapp's Garden," with its beautiful flowers and shrubbery, its winding walks, its cool and cosy arbors, its tempting fruits (the more tantalizing from the prohibition, " hands off") ; the fish pond in the midst of overhanging evergreens, and in its centre the round tower, from the top of which the band of music was wont to send forth its sweet strains upon the evening air. But most surprising of all was the Grotto, constructed on the Chinese principle of pleasing by contrast. You approach, by a narrow tangled path, a small rude structure, of the roughest stone, overgrown with wild vines, and with a door apparently of rough oak bark. You enter—and you stand in the midst of a beautiful min-

iature Grecian temple, with a life-sized piece of emble-
matic statuary before you, and the dates of the great
events in the Society's history conspicuously engraved
in niches around you.

It was with such things as these, in those palmy days,
that the taste of the Harmonists was cultivated, the
tedium of their monotonous life alleviated, and their
many visitors gratified. No wonder that romantically
disposed tourists spoke and wrote of the place as an
Arcadia.

It may be proper to introduce here the following
notice of the Society in 1826, by the Duke of Saxe
Weimar, who visited it in that year.

" At the inn, a fine large frame house, we were received by Mr. Rapp, the principal, at the head of the
community. He is a grey-headed and venerable old
man ; most of the members immigrated twenty-one years
ago from Würtemberg, along with him.

" The warehouse was shown to us, where the articles
made here for sale or use, are preserved, and I admired
the excellence of all. The articles for the use of the
Society are kept by themselves, as the members have
no private possessions, and everything is in common,
so must they, in relation to all their wants, be supplied
from the common stock. The clothing and food they
make use of is of the best quality. Of the latter,
flour, salt meat, and all long keeping articles, are
served out monthly ; fresh meat, on the contrary, is
distributed as soon as it is killed, according to the size
of the family, &c. As every house has a garden, each
family raises its own vegetables, and some poultry, and
each family has its own bake-oven. For such things

as are not raised in Economy, there is a store provided, from which the members, with the knowledge of the Directors, may purchase what is necessary, and the people of the vicinity may do the same.

" Mr. Rapp finally conducted us into the factory again, and said that the girls had especially requested this visit, that I might hear them sing. When their work is done they collect in one of the factory rooms, to the number of sixty or seventy, to sing spiritual and other songs. They have a peculiar hymn book, containing hymns from the old Würtemberg collection, and others written by the elder Rapp. A chair was placed for the old patriarch, who sat amidst the girls, and they commenced a hymn in a very delightful manner. It was naturally symphonious, and exceedingly well arranged. The girls sang four pieces, at first sacred, but afterward by Mr. Rapp's desire, of a gay character. With real emotion did I witness this interesting scene.

" Their factories and workshops are warmed during the winter by means of pipes connected with the steam engine. All the workmen, and especially the females, had very healthy complexions, and moved me deeply by the warm-hearted friendliness with which they saluted the elder Rapp. I was also much gratified to see vessels containing fresh sweet scented-flowers, standing on all the machines. The neatness which universally reigns, is in every respect worthy of praise."

But it is not to be wondered at that in such a community, where no provision is made for its perpetuation, where the young are growing old, and the old passing away, there should be a gradual decadence in taste and enterprise. The cotton, woolen, and silk manufactures were abandoned years ago—the last because it was not profitable, and all, because there was a lack of mechanical skill in those whose eyes now needed the aid of glasses and whose hands were becoming tremulous. Diminishing numbers also required more force to be applied to the culture of the ground. The museum was found to be an unprofitable investment, and it was sold at a sacrifice. Its mineralogical department, after remaining for a time in the custody of the Western Pennsylvania Hospital, was ultimately transferred to the Western University of Pennsylvania, at Pittsburgh, where its remains may still be seen. The deer were unprofitable stock, and the labyrinth was a toy, which only encumbered the ground where it stood. The Grotto has exchanged its old and proper thatch covering for a civilized roof. The old musicians of the band have relinquished their labor (except at religious festivals) to younger and less skillful hands, and the late efficient leader, having yielded to the power of the tender passion and gone in the ways of Hymen, is no longer a member of the Society.

The Economites have always excelled in the culture of the grape and the manufacture of wine. The vineyards, however, which they planted many years ago, have been abandoned, so far as field culture is concerned, and the grapes which they now use are supplied almost entirely from vines growing on their houses. The upper story of each house is covered on three sides with vines carefully trained on trellis work attached to the house; and besides the ornamental appearance of these vines, the grapes are found to be better protected from the frost, and more richly sweetened by the sun, than those grown elsewhere. For some years past, also, their finest wines have been produced from the common red currant, several acres of which are cultivated for this purpose. The grapes which they cultivate for wine have been chiefly the Catawba and Isabella, while they have not been inattentive to the claims of the new varieties.

In the year 1832, the Society suffered a diminution of one-third of its number, through the great secession under Count Leon, the history of which will be given in the next chapter.

CHAPTER V.

SECESSION UNDER COUNT DE LEON.

*HE OPENS CORRESPONDENCE WITH RAPP—CLAIMS A DI-
VINE MISSION—COMES TO ECONOMY—WISHES TO BE AT
THE HEAD OF AFFAIRS — DRAWS OFF A PARTY — THE
SOCIETY DIVIDED—COMPROMISE MADE—NEW SOCIETY
FORMED AT PHILLIPSBURG—CASH EXHAUSTED—COUNT
FAILS TO MAKE GOLD OUT OF ROCKS—MOB VISITS ECON-
OMY—DRUMMED OUT — BUBBLE BURSTS— COUNT TAKES
FRENCH LEAVE—DIES ON RED RIVER, &c.*

IN the year 1829, a long letter was received from
Frankfort-on-the-Main, purporting to be written
by John George Goentgen, Doctor of Philosophy and Theology, but who signs himself Samuel, this
being the name which he claims as belonging to him
under the new dispensation of which he writes. He
does not directly name the personage who afterward
called himself the Count De Leon, but refers to him
under such appellations as the Anointed of the Lord,
the Divine Messenger, &c., and speaks of him in terms
applicable only to the Messiah, whose second advent
was at that time daily expected by many among the
pietistic sects of Germany. Of this man's previous
history we have but little, except that his proper name
was Bernard Müller, and that he had gathered around
him at Frankfort, a religious sect of mystical and millennarian Pietists, who held him in high reverence,

under the name of Broli. He claimed to have a Divine commission to proclaim to the world the judgments which were impending in "the last days," and to call upon all the Lord's people to come out from among the wicked, and gather themselves together in some place where they might await the glorious personal advent of the Redeemer. He addressed a solemn circular, or letter apostolic, to the several courts and heads of churches in Europe, warning them of the coming judgments, and bidding them to publish this message, and not to interfere with the coming out of the Lord's people.

His letter to George Rapp, written by Göntgen, who seems to have been his amanuensis or private secretary, expresses great reverence for him and his Society, whom he professes to regard as the first fruits of the new millennial church, a portion of that body spoken of in the book of Revelation, chapter 12, as "the woman who fled into the wilderness where she hath a place prepared of God," &c. He expresses his belief that America is not included in the field upon which the prophetic judgments are to fall, but is to be the home of God's chosen ones, and that Rapp's Society are honored with being the forerunners of the church of the " first born," which is to be gathered into this land. He proposes to bring with him a company of his own followers, with a view either to joining themselves to the Harmony Society, or to the forming of a separate community on kindred principles, as might seem best. He inquires concerning the quality and price of lands, the eligibility of locations, &c. See Appendix E

From the pious tone of this letter, and the similarity of its sentiments to those of Rapp and his people, a favorable opinion was formed, and an encouraging answer was returned.   Nothing more, however, was heard from Leon until October, 1831, when a letter was received from him stating that he had just arrived in New York, with about forty persons, and desiring to know whether they could be accommodated at Economy during the winter.

Having received an affirmative answer, they came on immediately.   Leon, assuming an air of great dignity, sends forward two of his suite to herald his approach, he himself tarrying in the meantime in Pittsburgh.   A formal public reception was arranged for him.   The minds of the people having been prepared for some time before, by Rapp's preaching, for the advent of such a personage, it was a time of great expectations with the honest and simple-minded Harmonists.   As soon as the coach which bore Leon approached the town, it was greeted with a salute of the finest music from the band stationed on the tower of the church. The Count (*soi-disant*) was met at the hotel and escorted to the church, where the whole community are assembled awaiting his arrival.   He enters in state, attended by his Minister of Justice in full military garb, and sword at his side.   He is shown into the pulpit by Mr. Rapp, and all eyes are fixed upon him and all ears are open.   The great man stands before them !   But where are all his solemn prophetic utterances ?   Instead of delivering an address befitting the occasion, he only expresses his belief that " this meeting is the most important event since the creation, and that henceforth all the troubles and sorrows of the Lord's people will cease ;" and then professes to be too full of emotion for further utterance.   Mr. Rapp makes a brief address, in which he coolly expresses his doubts as to whether the happy period anticipated by the Count has yet arrived, and then dismisses the assembly.

Five houses were assigned to Leon and his followers, and a few boarded at the hotel, paying their own expenses.

As yet, Rapp and his people knew nothing of the views and character of these strangers, except what might be gathered from the letter above mentioned. Some of the more discerning ones, however, soon began to form unfavorable opinions from what they saw and heard.   Meetings for conference were held two or three evenings every week, for a month or more, between the leading men on both sides   Leon was heard at length in exposition of his views, and extended passages were read from a volume which he called the " Golden Book."   The conferences were not satisfactory.   The more Rapp learned of Leon's views, the more he disliked them.   Rapp's system aimed at the crucifixion of the flesh and separation from the spirit of the world.   He believed that religion required the bearing of the cross.   Leon seemed to think that the offense of the cross would cease under the new order of things which he was called to introduce.   He favored a better style of dress and living, and especially was he disposed to encourage matrimony among his followers. It was soon found that there could be no union between the two societies, and Leon and his party would have been expected to leave at once, but for the late-

ness and inclemency of the season. Being permitted
to remain through the winter, they had ample opportunities of mingling with the people in their manufactories, workshops, and elsewhere.

These opportunities were but too well employed in
fomenting dissatisfaction and discord. Leon was ex-
tolled by his friends as a man of extraordinary knowledge, experience, and wisdom, possessing even the art
of making gold out of the rocks around them. His
Divine commission was also urged, and the danger of
resisting his claims. Those whose ear could be gained
were invited to visit him at his house, and thus he
held his evening levees, and Absalom-like, endeavored
to steal away the hearts of the young and unstable
among the members. It was represented to them that
if Count Leon were their leader he would soon bring
the Society to a great state of advancement, giving
them better fare, better clothing, more personal
comforts, less work, and above all, the privilege of
marriage, so much desired by some. These seductive
representations were not without their effect upon some
of those who were not fully imbued with the principles
of the Society, especially the young, the disaffected, and
the recently admitted members. A paper was drawn
up and published in the newspapers, in which Leon
was mentioned as the future head and leader of the
association, and outstanding bills were to be sent in
to him for settlement. This paper was signed by all
those who favored his claims, to the number of two
hundred and fifty, including men, women, and children.
Another and counter paper was also prepared and
signed by those who were determined to adhere to the

old order of things, expressing confidence in their
present leaders and protesting against the divisive
movement.   This paper contained five hundred names,
and thus the Society stood divided two-thirds against
one-third.

A state of temporary anarchy ensued, and the Society seemed to be on the verge of dissolution.   Members of the same household took opposite sides.   It was
a trying time to the old and faithful members, whose
quiet habitations were now for the first time disturbed
with the noise of strife and contention.   But they
trusted in God and in their tried leaders, and they
determined to go forward.   The question now was,
how best to rid themselves of these treacherous guests
and their adherents ?   To wait the slow process of the
law would occupy too much time.   They determined
to make a compromise.   The terms, as finally agreed
upon and ratified on the 6th of March, 1832, in legal
form, were in substance these : The adherents of Leon,
now members of the Society, were to withdraw from it
and leave Economy, within three months; relinquish-
ing all claims whatever upon the property, money, and
real estate of the Society, and taking with them only
their personal clothing, household furniture, &c., in
consideration of the sum of one hundred and five thousand dollars, to be paid to them in three instalments
within the year.   Leon himself and suite were to leave
within six weeks.

With the money they received, the withdrawing
party purchased the village of Phillipsburg, on the
opposite side of the Ohio, ten miles below Economy,
with about eight hundred acres of land.   Here they

settled and organized themselves into a Society on the community principle, but allowing marriage. They called their association the New Philadelphia Society. They erected a hotel, factories, &c., and proposed to rival Economy in manufacturing, farming, vine raising, &c. In order to make good the promises of Leon as to better living, less work, &c., their expenditures for the first year far exceeded their income, including the amount paid them from Economy. Finding themselves largely in debt and their credit exhausted, they called upon the Count to bring into requisition his power of making gold; and he is said actually to have built a laboratory and made the attempt to extract gold from stones. A small portion of the precious metal at length appeared, but how it got into the crucible was not explained. The promised gold is not forthcoming, and the seceders, who had been made to believe that they were living on the Count's money, now find out that their own one hundred and five thousand dollars are expended, and they are indignant and much excited against his countship. In order to allay the rising tempest he persuades them to make an additional demand upon the Harmony Society, under the plea that too little had been paid them, and that he himself had never sanctioned the compromise.

Having little hope of extorting anything more by process of law, and being in need of the ready cash, they determined to adopt a summary process. On the second of April, 1833, a mob of about eighty persons entered the town of Economy, took forcible possession of the hotel, and then laid their demands before the authorities in a long and offensive document, which ended in terms similar to a declaration of war. This ultimatum was formally considered and promptly rejected, with the reply that the terms of the compromise which had been accepted by both parties had been fully complied with, and nothing more could be yielded. The members of the Society, meanwhile, all remained quietly in their houses, as they had been advised, so that there might be no collision. The mob then threatened loudly to enter Mr. Rapp's house by force, in order, as they alleged, to get possession of certain papers which would sustain their claims. But finding the house barricaded and well guarded from within, they desisted from the attempt. They gathered again around the hotel, and helped themselves freely to whatever provisions, liquors, &c., they could find.

In the meantime, many of the neighbors and friends of the Economites, hearing of the proceedings, had gathered in to see what was going on ; and after having learned the unreasonable demands of the mob, they sent for further assistance, and toward evening they rose up in a bold American way, under a dauntless leader, and drove the invaders from the town before drum and fife, and to the tune of the Rogue's March. During the whole day, however, not a drop of blood was shed, nor even a blow was struck.

The next morning complaint was made at Beaver, the county seat, against the individuals composing the mob, as well as against Leon and his associates, and they were bound over as conspirators to answer at the June court. Indictments were presented to the grand jury, and true bills found against the whole of them, but their attorneys managed to put off the trials to the

September term. Between June and September they had ample time to examine into the state of their affairs and learn their true position. The eyes of the misguided seceders were now thoroughly opened, and they thought it advisable to get rid of their bogus Count and prophet. He was accordingly, with a small number of his own followers, quietly shipped on board a keel-boat, and leaving his debts and legal recognizances for others to care for, he made the best of his way to Alexandria, on the Red river, in Louisiana, where he died of cholera, in the fall of 1833. He seems to have been a compound of the enthusiast and the impostor.

The seceders, being thus left to themselves, made an assignment, divided the property and debts *pro rata*, and started anew on the individual system. By calling into action the industry and carefulness which they had practiced at Economy, and improving each one his own allotted share of the land, they soon relieved themselves of their debts, and began to prosper. When the September term of the court came on, the Harmony Society, by advice of their lawyers, consented to withdraw the suits against their former brethren,—now that the maker of all the mischief was gone away in shame, —they paying all the costs. Thus the difficulties were ended, and thus ingloriously terminated all the splendid schemes of Herr Bernard Müller, Broli, Count de Leon, Divine Messenger, &c.

This diminution of their numbers by one-third, together with the amount of money paid to the seceders, might have been supposed to be a great loss to the Society. But it was, on the whole, a decided gain.

They were relieved from all the discordant materials which, in the course of time, had become intermingled with their organization. A greater measure of true harmony and brotherly love than they had known for years before, was now restored. They henceforth pursue the even tenor of their way in peace. All their enterprises prosper. The social machinery works smoothly, and they find verified in their experience the truth of a remark pithily made by one of their leaders, in view of the events above recorded, that " happiness is not always found in great numbers nor in large masses."

CHAPTER VI.

VARIOUS LAW SUITS.

*THE MÜLLER CASE— THE SCHRIBER CASE— THE NACH-
TRIEB AND LEMMIX CASES—EMINENT LEGAL TALENT
EMPLOYED, &c.*

HE Harmonists have never been a litigious people, but true to their name, they have aimed to
live in harmony with all men. They have not
been able, however, to escape altogether the necessity of
appealing unto Cæsar in defense of their rights. This
they have not done willingly, but in nearly all cases
have been the respondents in suits brought against them.
It is not proposed to notice these law-suits in detail.
To the more important of them lawyers have access in
the published reports, and the public generally would
not care to read of such things. They, however,
attracted much attention at the time, both from the
eminent legal talent employed, and from the importance of the principles involved; while to the Society
itself, they have been among the great events of its
history, breaking in upon the quiet and seclusion of
the peaceful community, and dragging them before the
great world. A brief notice of the principal ones
must suffice.

The first suit of which we have any notice was

brought by one Eugene Müller, who withdrew from the
Society about the year 1821–2, and removed to Pittsburgh. He was not one of the original members, and
was never in full harmony with the spirit of the organization. The suit was brought to recover wages for
labor and services rendered while a member of the
Society. As all such claim is formally renounced in
the articles of association, which Müller himself
had signed, he was easily defeated before the court.
Even had his cause been a good one, his chance of
success must have been small, when opposed by such
men as James Ross and John H. Hopkins (the latter
being now Senior Bishop of the Episcopal Church in
the United States, but then a member of the Pittsburgh bar).

Peter Schriber, with his five sons and four daughters, joined the Society in 1806, one year after its
organization. They did not come from Germany with
Mr. Rapp, but were originally from Adams county,
Pennsylvania, and had removed to Columbiana county,
Ohio. Here George Rapp became acquainted with
them in 1803, and enjoyed their hospitality while
exploring the Tuscarawas country in search of a place
of settlement for his people. Schriber was a man of
some wealth, owning one thousand acres of land, with
horses, stock, &c. He was a man of decided religious
character, and was so delighted with Rapp's plans for
the new religious society which he proposed to form,
that he determined to join the association as soon as it
should be fully organized. Accordingly, in 1806, he
left his farm in Ohio, and came with all his family and
a large amount of personal property to Harmony, Penn-

sylvania, where Rapp and his people had settled. All this property, together with the proceeds of the sale of his farm afterward, amounting in all to some eight thousand dollars, was thrown into the common stock of the Society, according to the terms of the original articles of association. All the Schriber family concurred in this action, and they continued to be faithful and contented members of the Society during life, except Jacob, the fourth son. This Jacob was a man of somewhat visionary and enthusiastic character, and was an eager advocate for the removal of the Society to the land of Palestine, there to await the Lord's coming. Not finding much sympathy with his views, and having come under some unfavorable influences (among others, probably that of the tender passion), he withdrew in 1826, and returned to Ohio.

Here he met with sever:l other dissatisfied seceding members, with whom he held frequent conferences. Finding that they had grievances in common, and having but little hope from the courts, they prepared a memorial to the Legislature of Pennsylvania, which was extensively signed by seceding members and others, asking for a committee of investigation to examine into the affairs of the Harmony Society, with a view to the redress of alleged wrongs and grievances. The memorial was referred to the judiciary committee, who reported that the allegations of the memorialists were improbable and not sustained by evidence, and referred them to the courts for an adjustment of their pecuniary claims.

After the death of his father Peter Schriber, who being a member of the Society had died intestate,

Jacob, as one of the surviving heirs, took out letters of administration, and made a demand upon the Society for an account of the property of his father in their hands. Suit was brought before Judge Bre lin, of the Court of Common Pleas of Beaver county, who decided adversely to the claim. An appeal was taken to the Supreme Court of Pennsylvania, where the judgment of the lower court was affirmed, after an able opinion by Judge Gibson, which is recorded in Watts' Reports, vol. 5, p. 360–4.

The legal principles decided by this trial were, 1st, "that an association by which each surrendered his property into one common stock, for the mutual benefit of all, during their joint lives, with the right of survivorship, reserving to each the privilege to secede at any time during his life, is not prohibited by law. And that right of secession is not transmissible to the personal representative of a party to such agreement, so as to enable him to recover the property of his intestate, so put into the common stock." 2d. That "a member of a religious society cannot avoid a contract with it on the basis of its peculiar faith, by setting up the supposed extravagance of its doctrines as a proof that he was entrapped." The attorneys for the Society in this case were Richard Biddle and Walter Forward, both afterward among the distinguished men of the nation.

The Nachtrieb case was a bill in equity filed by Joshua Nachtrieb, before the Circuit Court of the United States for the Western District of Pennsylvania, at the November term of 1849; in which it is charged, that the complainant having been a member of the Society, was unjustly excluded and deprived of any participation in the property and benefits of the association, and praying for an account of the property and effects at the time of his exclusion, and that his share be awarded to him by decree of the court. This was a protracted case, and was managed by distinguished counsel on both sides, the attorneys for the complainant being Charles Shaler, Edwin M. Stanton and Th. Umbstaetter; for the Society, A. W. Loomis and Wilson M'Candless.

During the years 1850 and 1851, a great mass of testimony was taken in various places, by commissioners appointed by the court, and the case was argued at the November term, 1851, before Judges Grier and Irwin, who, after a full hearing, took the case under advisement, and on the 5th of April, 1852, delivered their opinion, sustaining the claim of the complainant. The Trustees of the Harmony Society, R. L. Baker and J. Henrici, were ordered to render a full account of the net value of all the estate of the Society during the twenty-seven years of the complainant's membership, in order that the court might determine the amount due to him as his proper share of the whole. This led to a protracted and tedious investigation before Commissioner Henry Sproul, in which the pecuniary affairs of the Society, from the very beginning, were minutely and inquisitorially examined into, and all their books and accounts, their methods of transacting business, the value of their lands and all other possessions, were brought under review. The final result was the issuing of a decree in 1855 by Judge Grier, awarding **to the complainant the sum** of three thousand eight hundred and ninety dollars, as his rightful share in the estate of the Society. The operation, however, of this decree was suspended by an appeal which was taken by the Society to the Supreme Court of the United States. At the December term of 1856, the case was finally adjudicated by a reversal of the decree of the lower court, Justice Campbell pronouncing the judgment of this high tribunal in an ably written opinion. Thus Nachtrieb was defeated, and this "seven years' war" was ended.

It was a hard case for the complainant, and public sympathy was very much in his favor, inasmuch as it appeared plainly in the course of the trial that his alleged *voluntary withdrawal* from the Society, which was plead as a bar to his claim, was virtually an *expulsion* by the authority of George Rapp. His offense, too, which was holding conversation by appointment with some of the Phillipsburgers, was regarded as a trivial one, by those who were not acquainted with the true state of things at Economy. But Nachtrieb was known by the leaders to be a disaffected and unsound member, and to be in sympathy with those hostile seceders, who were still plotting against the Society, and were reported as having threatened the destruction of the town. In these circumstances a favorable opportunity only was wanting to bring such a pressure to bear upon the offender as to *constrain* his voluntary withdrawal, and thus rid the Society of an undesirable member. His signing of a paper in which he declares " I have this day withdrawn myself from the Harmony Society, and ceased to be a member thereof," and acknowledges the " receipt of two hundred dollars as a donation according to contract," was regarded by the Supreme Court as conclusive evidence against his alleged expulsion, and as a bar to all claims.

Elijah Lemmix was the friend and associate of Nachtrieb, and left the Society at the same time, and under the same circumstances, except that his withdrawal was more manifestly a voluntary one than that of Nachtrieb. In 1852, after the decision of Judges Grier and Irwin in favor of Nachtrieb, Lemmix also brought suit before the same court, for the recovery of his share of the property. A similar course of protracted investigation was had, under the management of the same able attorneys; but at the February term of the court, in 1855, Judge Irwin pronounced a brief and decided opinion adverse to the claim of the petitioner. Thus Lemmix, also, was defeated, and at the same time an effectual estoppal was put to a series of annoying law suits about to be entered by seceding members, which, had they been successful, must have resulted in the entire dissolution of the Society.

It was found, by the investigation into the actual wealth of the Society before Commissioner Sproul, that instead of some eight or ten millions, at which the property was wildly estimated by the complainants, it did not amount in all to quite one million; and in order to meet the demands of all who would have been encouraged to make similar claims against the Society, this million of dollars would soon have been exhausted, and the remaining members left penniless.

These law suits had been extremely vexatious. All the private and domestic concerns of the Society were pried into, all their branches of business and the profits of each, all their religious and social usages, everything, indeed, which was *nobody's business but their own*, was impertinently, needlessly, and inquisitorially dragged into public view. The result of the whole, however, was to the benefit and credit of the Society. They became better known and understood; the extravagant estimates of their supposed wealth no longer awakened jealousy; and especially, the unimpeachable integrity with which their financial affairs had been managed by the leaders, even though never called to account by the Society, was a refreshing exhibition of honesty in the use of funds which is but too rarely found.

CHAPTER VII.

ITS LATER HISTORY.

*CHANGE IN ONE OF THE ARTICLES OF ASSOCIATION—
OUTSIDE ENTERPRISES— THEY OWN TWO RAILROADS
AND A TOWN—THEIR OIL BUSINESS, &c.*

ACCORDING to the original articles of association, assented to at the organization of the Society in 1805, and more formally adopted at New Harmony, Indiana, in 1821, and renewed again at Economy, Pennsylvania, in 1827, it was stipulated that in case of the *withdrawal* of any member of the Society, for any cause, the money or property originally brought into the common fund by such person, should be *refunded* without interest, in one, two, or three annual instalments. This provision had been found, at a very early period, to operate unfavorably, both by keeping up a feeling of inequality among the members, according as they had brought in less or more into the Society, and by fostering a disposition to withdraw among any who might become disaffected. Accordingly, as early as 1818, those who had been among the original members, agreed by common consent to *destroy* the record which had been kept of the amount contributed by each, in order that their children might not know, and that they themselves might forget, as far as possible, how much each family had brought in. It was not, however, until after some of the lawsuits before described, and especially after the difficulties growing out of the claims of Count Leon's adherents, that it was determined to abrogate altogether the article which provided for refunding to withdrawing members. Accordingly in 1836 the following new articles were unanimously adopted and signed by the three hundred and ninety-one members, then composing the Society, viz.: " 1st. The said sixth article [in regard to refunding] is entirely annulled and made void, as if it had never existed, all others to remain in full force as heretofore. 2d. All the property of the Society, real, personal and mixed, in law or equity, and howsoever contributed or acquired, shall be deemed now and forever, joint and indivisible stock. Each individual is to be considered to have finally and irrevocably parted with all his former contributions, whether in lands, goods, money or labor, and the same rule shall apply to all future contributions, whatever they may be. 3d. Should any individual withdraw from the Society, or depart this life, neither he in the one case, nor his representatives in the other, shall be entitled to demand an account of said contributions, or to claim anything from the Society as a matter of right. But it shall be left altogether to the discretion of the superintendent to decide whether any, and if any, what allowance shall be made to such member, or his representatives, as a donation." See Appendix D.

These new articles effectually precluded all further claims from any who might withdraw, and made it the common interest of all alike to live and die in fellowship with the Society. It has always been customary, however, to make a donation to any member who withdraws in an open, regular manner, to the amount usually of not less than two hundred dollars; and in special cases a much larger amount has been granted.

The later years of the Society's history up to the present time are marked by few incidents worthy of notice. They have continued to pursue the same quiet and industrious course of life as in former years. All their business is conducted with clock-work regularity. There is a place for everything, and everything is in its place. Every individual has his or her proper work to do, and all go forth to their daily employments with apparent cheerful contentment. To the eye of a stranger, the town has a dull and *finished* appearance. Its grass-grown streets, its Sabbath stillness, and the absence of children (except a few apprentices and others), render it all unlike most other American towns. There are many transient visitors, who are hospitably entertained at the hotel, but no regular boarders are received as in former years. Owing to diminishing numbers, they have necessarily contracted the range of their mechanical and agricultural operations, and their profits from these sources are proportionately diminished. They keep a store, which serves for the accommodation of themselves and their neighbors, and where is also the postoffice, and the general place of business for the Trustees.

Accumulation is no longer among the prominent aims of the Society. They have enough for their own wants, and have no need to lay up for others. A certain portion, however, of their capital must be kept employed. Among their chief sources of income, for some years past, have been certain outside enterprises, especially the oil business. But even into these investments they have been drawn involuntarily, rather than from the prevalent spirit of speculation by which others are influenced.

They have ever been ready to extend aid and relief to individuals and enterprises which commanded their confidence, not forgetful at the same time of the safety of the investments which they were called to make. In this way they have often been compelled to become the sole owners of property which they did not want, in order to save themselves from loss through the failure of the parties to whom they had advanced funds. In some such cases, especially where an individual or family were concerned, they have waited long and patiently for payments due, and have given every opportunity to their debtors to recover from their embarrassments, and to redeem property which had been mortgaged to the Society. Many a family in Beaver and Allegheny counties, and elsewhere, are now in comfortable circumstances or even wealthy, who would have been utterly bankrupt but for the forbearance of these benevolent creditors.

Where companies have been concerned, while they have been forbearing, they have also, as in duty bound, had an eye to profitable returns. All loans and other investments have been in the hands of the Trustees, who as faithful business managers, were bound to consult the interests of the Society. Sometimes they had found an *elephant* on their hands, and sometimes they have hit upon a good speculation.

Among their larger outside investments may be mentioned the Saw-Mill Run coal mines and railroad, once a single interest under one company, but now divided, the Economites still retaining a large share in the stock of the railroad, partly for the relief of the company and partly for the value of the investment.

They are also now sole owners of a railroad some six miles long, which connects with the Pittsburgh, Fort Wayne and Chicago railway at Darlington, in Beaver county, Pennsylvania, and extends to a tract of land of about one thousand acres, containing valuable mines of bituminous and cannel coal. In order to facilitate the sale of this property, they are now boring for oil on this land, it being only a few miles from the great Island Run oil region. If they succeed in striking oil, they will benefit both themselves and the owners of adjoining tracts, and if they fail they are able to bear the loss.

The town of Old Brighton (now called Beaver Falls), containing some five hundred acres of land, now laid out in town lots, together with one of the finest water-powers in the country, belongs to the Society, it having fallen into their hands in the way indicated above. They are now selling out the lots and water-power privileges, at low rates, for the accommodation of those whose means are limited.

But their largest and most profitable outside investment is a large tract of land, of some six thousand acres, opposite Tidioute, in Warren county, Pennsylvania. This was originally purchased as a lumber region, for the supply of their own wants and to meet the extensive demand for lumber which is made at their saw-mill in Economy. Connected with this original tract is another smaller body of land, which they took originally in payment of a bad debt, and also for its lumber.

This latter tract has since proved to be a valuable oil territory, and it is here that the Society now owns several fine wells, which have been a large source of income for the last four years. When the oil was first discovered, as it was a great and unexpected addition to the value of the land, they generously intrusted the management of it to the former proprietor, with such a share in the profits as enabled him to retrieve his shattered fortune and place his family in independent circumstances. They then took the whole business into their own hands.

What may be the present value of the entire estate and possessions of the Society, and how large their annual income, the writer has not troubled himself particularly to inquire, nor does it concern the great public to be more definitely informed. Nor has it been deemed necessary to indulge in any curious speculation in regard to the question which every one is ready to ask, but which no one can answer, namely: What is to become of all this property after the present members of the Society shall have passed away? Some of them expect, even yet, that the Lord will come in his glory before they are all gone. Those who live long enough will see.

CHAPTER VIII.

RELIGION OF THE HARMONISTS.

MYSTICO-PIETISTIC—NOT A SECT—COMMUNITY OF GOODS —DUALISM OF ADAM—HOW HE FELL—PHILOSOPHY OF CELIBACY—FALL OF LUCIFER—MYSTICAL COSMOGONY— FINAL RESTITUTION OF ALL THINGS.

THE religious opinions of the Harmonists have been very cursorily noticed in the preceding chapters. The popular misconceptions on this subject are so great, that a more full discussion seems desirable. As they acknowledge no written creed but the Bible itself, it is the more difficult to secure any correct or closely defined statement of their religious views. They may be regarded as among the offshoots of Pietism in its later developments, embracing also a good deal of the mystic element. They reverence the names of Arndt, Spener, and Franke, but their views more closely assimilate to those of Böhm, Arnold, Petersen, Bengel, and Jung Stilling. They are very decided Trinitarians, and highly exalt the character of Jesus Christ, making him all in all in their system of salvation. They formerly kept up a friendly correspondence with the Shakers, who resemble them in the matter of community of goods and of celibacy, but they lately declined any further intercourse, on the ground

of some heretical publications of the Shakers in regard
to the divinity of Christ.   They are not, however,
intolerant or denunciatory toward other Christian de-
nominations, whether Catholic or Protestant, but they
are decided in maintaining their own views, which are
rather practical than dogmatic.   A " total regeneration
of the heart through the mercy and grace of our
Saviour," they regard as necessary to enable us to put
in practice the simple but all-important principles of
the religion of Christ, which they attempt to carry out
in their peculiar organization and mode of life.   "Love
to God above all and to thy neighbor as thyself, without laying much stress on forms, letter or ceremony,"
they give as " constituting the sum and substance of
their religious creed."   They do not regard themselves
as a distinct religious sect, and they have no ecclesiastical organization apart from the civil community.   In
this respect their system is strictly *patriarchal*, while,
at the same time, they constitute a voluntary association, in which all who are permitted to sub-
scribe to their articles of agreement become entitled
alike to all the civil and all the religious privileges of
the Society.   They are governed, as has been stated,
by a board of nine elders, chosen by themselves, two
of which elders are appointed and designated as Trustees, and are *ex-officio* the business managers and
religious leaders of the community.

Their system of community of goods was originally
adopted, and is still maintained, mainly from religious
motives.   They refer for authority to the example of
the primitive Christians, as recorded in Acts 4 : 32, &c.,
" And the multitude of them that believed were of one

heart and of one soul: neither said any of them that aught of the things which he possessed was his own; but they had all things common." This they regard as not having been a temporary arrangement, but a normal principle in the organization of the Christian church. They shared this opinion in common with some of the other separatists of Germany, and though perhaps unwittingly, they imitated the very ancient example of the Greek Pythagoras, and of the Jewish Essenes. See Appendix C.

THE DUAL ADAM.—Their views in regard to the original character of Adam are peculiar. They believe him to have been created in the exact image of God, and in a higher and more mystical sense than is commonly attached to those words. Instead of confining the image of God to a mere moral likeness in " knowledge, righteousness, and holiness," they include in it also a resemblance in form to the person of the God-man, or God-manifest, whose " voice was heard walking in the garden," and whose visible appearances are often referred to in the Old Testament; this theanthropic manifestation being not merely anticipative of his incarnation, when he was " made in the likeness of man," but his original and normal characteristic as the Logos or God-revealed. Hence the expression, " No man hath seen God at any time ; the only begotten Son, who is in the bosom of the Father, he hath declared (revealed) him." His incarnation as the son of Mary was but the subjection of his theanthropic person to all the conditions of our fallen humanity, " without sin." Thus he became the second Adam.

Man they regard as constituting the highest order of

created beings, higher even than the angels, who are only " ministering spirits sent forth to minister to the heirs of salvation." This they infer also from his being the last in the ascending order of creation, as well as from the honor put upon our humanity through its assumption by Christ as the second Adam, who " took not on him the nature of angels." The passage which says, " Thou hast made him a little lower than the angels," they understand as it is given in Luther's version, " Thou hast for a little time deprived him of the angels," *i. e.*, in the person of Christ, as " Son of man," who during his incarnation was deprived of that ministry and worship of angels with which he was surrounded before he became man.

They regard Adam also as having been made a *dual being*, having both the sexual elements within himself, according to Gen. 1:26, 27, " And God said, Let us make man in our image, after our likeness, and let *them* have dominion," &c. And " so God created man in his own image ; in the image of God created he him ; male and female created he them." They understand the word *them* in both these verses as applying to the dual Adam, before the separation of Eve from him, as recorded in the second chapter.

ADAM'S FALL.—This separation also they regard as a consequence of the incipient fall of Adam, which took place at the time when the various animals were caused to pass before him, and when, beholding them all in pairs, he conceived a desire for a similar separation and companionship in his own case, thus becoming discontented with the condition in which God had placed him, and abusing his freedom of will by yielding to his lower animal nature. The restlessness and worry of mind thus induced was a physical cause of the deep sleep that fell upon him, and that resulted in the separation of the female sexual element from his person. The partaking together of the forbidden fruit was but the consummation and natural consequence of that earlier incipient apostacy. This view is supposed to be corroborated by the statement in Gen. 2:18, "The Lord God said, It is not good that the man should be alone." At the close of the six days' work, as recorded in ch. 1:31, all things were pronounced " very good," but now there is something that " is not good." How could man's loneliness, they ask, have become an evil (which before was "very good"), had he not already brought himself into a state of restlessness and dissatisfaction, which made it "not good" that he should be alone. God, therefore, allowed his fall to be complete by giving him a "help-meet for him" in his present deteriorated condition ; just as he afterward gave the Jews a king when they demanded it. Adam had conceived an irregular desire toward the feminine element of his nature, while it was yet a part of himself, and now that the woman has become a separate being, she readily completes the temptation, by presenting to him the forbidden fruit. This fruit they regard as an objective reality, and as possessing some sort of poisonous quality which introduced the seeds of disease and death into the human frame, and induced that unholy sexual passion which is implied in the discovery of their nakedness and the awakening of the sense of shame. The tree of life, on the other hand, they suppose would have been the means of sustaining man's physical immortality, if he had not fallen. This view seems to be sustained by Gen. 3 : 22, &c.

In regard to the command, " be fruitful and multiply," &c., as given in Gen. 1 : 28 (and as they say, before the separation of the sexual elements), they do not pretend to explain *how* this increase of the race could have been brought about; but they believe that it would have taken place in a manner incomprehensible to us, by a certain holy commingling of the male and female elements of man's being, at particular times, and with God's immediate approbation ; so that a new being would be in some way developed from man's person without physical pain. Such an offspring would have been truly a Son of God, as well as a Son of man, even as Jesus the son of Mary was. The person of Jesus they suppose to have been physically the same with that of Adam before his fall, *i. e. dual ;* the bodies of the risen saints (in the first resurrection) will be of the same physical conformation, and therefore, like the angels, incapable of marrying and giving in marriage. Matt. 22 : 30.

PHILOSOPHY OF CELIBACY.—We thus have a profound (though somewhat mystical) basis for their notions in regard to marriage and celibacy. Since man has fallen, and the sexual elements have become separated, contrary to God's original design, they regard all intercourse of the sexes as polluting ; and while it may be tolerated in lawful marriage, so far (and only so far,) as may be necessary for the perpetuation of the race, yet the offspring are all necessarily conceived in sin. Adam, after his fall, " begat a son in his own likeness" (not after the image of God), and such have been all his sinful posterity. Joseph, the husband of Mary, being a sinful man, could not beget a holy seed, and hence the necessity of the miraculous conception of Jesus, in order that he might be a Son of God, and free from the taint of ordinary generation. With these views, while they do not condemn marriage in those who choose to enter into that bond, they do, nevertheless, regard the celibate state as more pure and holy; more acceptable to God, and as better fitting them for that higher resurrection state which their millennarian views lead them to expect. And in support of this belief, they refer to those various passages of Scripture which have been cited in former chapters. They admit, also, that this celibate life is only suited to those who have a special vocation to it, according to our Saviour's words in Matthew 19 : 11, 12, " All men cannot receive this saying, save they to whom it was given. He that is able to receive it, let him receive it." If they be inquired of as to the probable consequences if mankind generally should be persuaded to adopt their practice on this subject, they will only reply, that the way would thus be the sooner prepared for the Lord's coming, and for the new heaven and new earth wherein shall dwell righteousness. Under that new and more glorious dispensation, they look for that literal " restitution of all things" to their primitive condition, which seems to be foretold ; when sin, pain, and death shall cease, and God will in truth dwell with men again, conversing with them face to face, as He did in Paradise.

MYSTICAL COSMOGONY.—They regard the present disordered condition of our earth in which the " whole creation groaneth and travaileth in pain together until now," as a consequence of the introduction of sin. The fall of Lucifer from his first estate, resulted from his being "lifted up with pride," and aiming at independence of God. On being banished, with his hosts, from heaven by the assault of Michael and his angels, he threw that part of the universe which he had before governed, into conflagration and chaos, such as this globe is represented to have been at the time when the six days' work begins. The world was without form and void (Heb. *tohu va vohu*), *i. e.* in a state of utter chaotic confusion, such as would be the result of that terrible satanic conflagration which was quenched by the waters that Michael poured upon the burning world. Thus the earth is found "standing out of the water and in the water," and all those igneous formations of which the geologists tell us are in a measure accounted for. Our globe has never recovered from its semi-chaotic condition. Its volcanoes, its earthquakes, its tornadoes, its pestilences, &c., are all so many throes of pain and travail under which it still "groaneth." A paradise was indeed prepared for man on a limited part of this stricken earth, and had he continued holy, this paradise would have been enlarged as might be necessary, until it should become like what the new heavens and the new earth will be hereafter. Had man not sinned, he would have eaten lawfully of the tree of life, and would have "lived for ever" in his earthly paradise, or been translated, as was Enoch, to a higher sphere. But now the earth is a fit habitation only for a fallen, sinful race of beings, "waiting," however, as the apostle says (Rom. 8 : 19), " with earnest expectation for the manifestation of the sons of God." It has been "subjected to vanity, in hope of being delivered from the bondage of corruption into the glorious liberty of the sons of God."

Man (the *microcosm*) has, by his apostacy, shared in the same ruin and awaits the same deliverance from the bondage of corruption, with the earth (the *macrocosm*) itself. His body has become subject to disease and death, his understanding is darkened, and his whole nature is fleshly. The apostle says, " even we ourselves, groan within ourselves, waiting for the adoption, to wit, the redemption of our body." Rom. 8 : 23. They teach, however, that as the earth itself still retains much of its pristine beauty and glory, so also in man's fallen nature there is much to remind him that he was made in God's image ; and that in every man, even the most degraded, there still remains a certain germ or " *sperm*"* of his original divinity which tends to germinate heavenward. Thus in all his darkness he yearns for the light, and sometimes " searches and feels after God, if haply he may find him." Yet such is the ascendency of evil, that even the " light which is in him is darkness," and it is only by a great regeneration-work that he can come fully " out of darkness into God's marvelous light." They do not, however, apply the term *regeneration*, as orthodox divines do, to a moment of incipient impulse toward goodness produced by the Spirit of God, but to the *entire process of man's recovery*, and the restoration of his " whole soul, body and spirit" to the image and favor of God. This is a work which is only in

* They term it also a *divine spark*.

part accomplished in this world ; the whole process will be complete only "in *the regeneration*, when the Son of man shall sit on the throne of his glory," &c., Matt. 19 : 28. Thus earth and man alike await the second advent of Him who will come to " destroy the works of the devil," and to restore the universe, both of matter and spirit, to its pristine purity and happiness. And in some far distant geological cycle, it may be, they expect that this great redemptive restoration-work will be consummated in the final removal of all sin and all suffering from the universe of God! Surely these are glorious dreams—if dreams they be.

CHAPTER IX.

RELIGION OF THE HARMONISTS.
(*Continued.*)

MILLENNARIAN VIEWS—ALLEGORICAL INTERPRETATION —RELIGIOUS USAGES—FUNERALS—CONCLUSION.

THEIR MILLENNARIAN VIEWS have often been alluded to in the preceding chapters, but no formal statement has been given of the particular phase of millennarianism which they embrace, or of the arguments by which they support it. We shall here notice these briefly.

Their belief in the ultimate restoration of this earth to its original paradisaic condition, as above alluded to, is founded not only upon the general principles which they hold in regard to the nature of God's redemptive work, as embracing the material as well as the spiritual universe, but also upon such specific declarations of Scripture as are found in Acts 3 : 20, 21, and Rom. 8 : 19–23. The former of these passages they connect also with Acts 1 : 11, " Ye men of Galilee, why stand ye gazing up into heaven? this same Jesus which is taken up from you into heaven, *shall so come in like manner* as ye have seen him go into heaven." This personal and visible return of Christ to this world they regard as referred to in the other passage, where the apostle Peter speaks of the " times of refreshing from the presence of the Lord," which shall be experienced " when he shall send Jesus Christ, whom the heaven must receive, until the *time of restitution of all things,* which God hath spoken by the *mouth of all his holy prophets* since the world began." Also in Rom 8 : 19, &c., where " the whole creation" is represented as " groaning and travailing in pain together," and waiting in earnest expectation for the manifestation of the sons of God, when " the *creation itself shall be delivered from the bondage of corruption,* into the glorious liberty of the children of God."   In this restitution of all things, they include not only (1st) the physical renovation of this disordered mundane system, and the introduction of the " new heavens and new earth" spoken of by the apostle Peter in his second Epistle, ch. 3 : 13, but also (2d) the restoration of the Jewish nation to the land of Palestine, according to the numerous ·predictions of the prophets to that effect (*e. g.* see Ezek. 37 : 21, Amos 9 : 11–15, Jer. 30 : 3, &c.), and (3d) their conversion to Christianity, according to Zech. 12 : 10, &c., " they shall look upon me whom they have pierced," &c., and Rom. 9 : 12–32, " and so all Israel shall be saved," &c.; and (4th) the resurrection of the sainted dead, and the transfiguration of the pious living, spoken of by the apostle Paul in 1 Thess. 4 : 13–18.   All this they regard as included in that universal " restitution," which is to be effected at the visible " appearing" of Him, whom the heaven was to receive until that time.

All this too, they expect to take place, not as perhaps most Christians do, at the final winding up of this world's affairs, before the great day of judgment, but at the *beginning* of the "thousand years," during which the saints are to live and reign with Christ, according to Rev. 20 : 4, 5, &c. This is that "first resurrection" in which they expect the risen and transfigured saints to be fully restored to the image of God by being clothed in bodies like unto Christ's glorious body, and like to the *dual* organization of Adam, when he first left the Creator's hand.

They believe also, that under the glorious kingdom of the Messiah, then to be set up, there will still be a *race of men in the flesh*, as at present, but who will " be all righteous" (Isa. 60 : 21), the kingdoms of the world having become the kingdoms of the Lord, &c. They look also for a literal realization, during this period, of that happy state foretold by the prophets, when the curse that was put upon the ground for man's sake, filling it with thorns and thistles, &c., shall be removed, and " instead of the thorn, shall come up the fir tree, and instead of the briar, the myrtle tree," &c.—when " they shall build houses and inhabit them, and they shall plant vineyards and eat the fruit of them"—when " the wolf and the lamb shall feed together, and the lion shall eat straw like the ox, and the little child shall lay its hand upon the cockatrice's den," &c.—when " there shall be *no more curse*," and " *no more death*." Instead of death will be *transfiguration* (like that of Enoch and Elijah), as fast as any shall have made such progress in holiness as to be prepared for this exaltation. Thus they would be prepared to accept as expressive of their views the following eloquent passage from Dr. Seiss' " Last Times," p. 207 :

" But Jerusalem below, radiant in all its untold glory, shall be but a type and earthly picture of the higher and sublimer Jerusalem that is above; that firmly-founded city for which Abraham looked, ' whose builder and maker is God'—that city which John saw ' descending out of heaven from God, having the glory of God, and light like unto a stone most precious, even like a jasper-stone, clear as crystal.' The one is earthly, the other is heavenly. The one is built by human hands, the other is the workmanship of God himself. The one has a population composed of men holy and happy, but men *in the flesh;* the other is the glorious residence of the glorified saints. The one shall rest upon the earthly mount, the other shall be 'above the mountains and the hills.' The one will need clouds and rain, sunshine and peaceful night, the other ' has no need of the sun nor of the moon to shine in it, for the glory of God shall lighten it, and the Lamb is the light thereof.' The one shall have its temple and its altars, the other ' has no temple therein, for the Lord God Almighty and the Lamb are the temple of it.' And whilst the sons of Abraham in the flesh shall possess Jerusalem that is below, the sons of Abraham by faith in Christ, ' who have come out of great tribulation, and washed their robes and made them white in the blood of the Lamb,' shall, in their glorification, have their everlasting bliss and home in ' the Jerusalem that is above.' The relation of the one to the other, is like that of the Sanctuary to the Holy of Holies. The one is the metropolis of the ' new earth,' the other of the ' new heavens.' The one is suspended in the clouds to pour its radiance on the saved nations below (Rev. 21 : 24), but both belong to the one sublime and wonderful economy which is to encompass this planet, when once its redemption is complete."

As to the precise date of this glorious appearing of Christ in his kingdom, they have learned to speak more cautiously than Father Rapp did during his lifetime. They have learned that it is "not for us to know the times or the seasons which the Father has put in his own power" (Acts 1 :7). They are inclined however, to assent to the theory most generally adopted in ancient times by Jewish Rabbis and Christian fathers, that the millennium will be the *seventh thousand years*, or great *Sabbath* of the world ; the golden period of *rest* to this sin-wearied earth, like unto the "rest" into which God entered after the six days' work of creation. They do not, however, pretend to judge as to the correctness of the various systems of chronology. They regard rather our Lord's injunction to his disciples, to "watch and pray," for "in such an hour as ye think not, the Son of man cometh "—and " ye know not when the time is."

Entertaining such expectations as these, it is not surprising that they should manifest so little anxiety about the future disposal of their earthly possessions. These may all be needed in that better state, when "*holiness* to the Lord shall be written even on the bells of the horses."*

* The recent success of the Atlantic Cable, and the prospect of the speedy completion of the Russo-American Telegraph by way of Behring's Straits, have lately recalled to their remembrance a remarkable prediction made by the celebrated *Nicolaus von der Flue*, hermit of Switzerland, who lived one hundred years before Luther. This man has a very interesting history, which need not be given here. He was

ALLEGORICAL INTERPRETATION.—The Sabbath dis-
courses of their leaders are not, as has been sometimes
alleged, made up largely of instructions in regard to
their secular affairs, but are decidedly biblical and religious. In their expositions of the Scriptures, especially of the Old Testament, they make much use of the
allegorical method. While not denying the literal verity of the historical facts, they seek a deeper typical or
symbolical meaning beneath the surface; and thus they
spiritualize the letter, and find the Old Testament full
of the richest gospel truth. In defense of this practice they appeal to the example of our Saviour himself
and his apostles, who thus spiritualize the "manna,"
and the "rock," and the "passover," and the "tabernacle," and "Mt. Sinai," &c.

To give a few examples : They regard the process of
creation—the "spirit of God moving upon the face of
the waters" (or chaos), the breaking in of "light"
through the thick darkness, &c., as symbolizing the
new creation, when "God who commanded the light
to shine out of darkness, shines in our hearts," &c.;
and the purifying *fires* of the final conflagration, which
shall prepare the way for the "new heavens and the

celebrated for his piety and wisdom, and was an expectant of the
Lord's coming; but when inquired of as to the probable *date* of this
great event, his only reply was, that *the Lord would come when a cord
should be put around the whole world!* The tradition of this enigmatical
prophecy is still prevalent in Switzerland. What the hermit may have
meant by it, is doubtful. But the probable completion of telegraphic
communication round the globe within the coming year, together
with the calculations of many interpreters of prophecy which fix the
date of the great consummation to the year 1866, or 1867, is at least a
striking coincidence. We are also reminded of Matt. 24:27, "As the
lightning cometh out of the east, and shineth unto the west, so shall
also, the coming of the Son of man be."

new earth," as resembling that "*baptism of fire*" by which Christ will burn up the "wood, hay, and stubble" of his people here, through various fiery processes, and will make even the "fires of hell" (as they suppose) a means of ultimate purification to lost souls !

Again, they take Moses as the representative of the *law*, and Joshua of the *gospel*. The exclusion of Moses from the promised land, was not merely a punishment for his offense in smiting the rock (which would have seemed too severe), but a great symbolical lesson to Israel, that salvation or entrance into the "*rest* that remaineth for the people of God," the heavenly Canaan, is not by the law, but by the gospel of Jesus, who is the Joshua of the New Testament. Comp. Heb. 4 : 8, " For if Jesus (*i. e.* Joshua,) had given them rest, then would he not have spoken of another day."

Thus also Noah, Joseph, and Boaz, are types of Christ; the "scarlet line in the window" of the harlot (hostess) Rahab, symbolizes the blood of Christ; and the year of jubilee, when all bondmen were liberated and every Israelite restored to his lost inheritance, but foreshadowed the great redemptive work of Christ under the gospel, and the great final Jubilee of the universe, when all the enthralled and banished "sons of God," both angelic and human, shall recover their lost inheritance in the kingdom of God !

It is not considered necessary to enter more largely upon the exposition of their religious views. On the various other points of Christian theology, they do not seem to differ materially from the Lutheran and other Protestant confessions. They are certainly not Calvinists, and their whole style of religious thought and

expression differs much from that of Scotland ; nevertheless they will admit, summarily, that the substitu-
tionary atoning sacrifice of Christ is their only ground
of hope for salvation, and a personal interest in this
great atonement is to be attained only by a living faith,
which brings the soul into fellowship with God, and
manifests itself in a holy life.

RELIGIOUS USAGES.—As to their outward religious
observances, they keep the Sabbath holy by abstaining
from ordinary and unnecessary labor, and by assembling twice for public worship, which is conducted very
much as that of other Protestants, with singing, prayer,
a sermon, &c. They, however, follow the example of
the Germans generally, in paying less regard to Sunday evening as holy time ; and their band of music in
years past was often heard sending forth its soft strains
from some secluded spot, as the sun went down.

Besides the religious observance of Christmas, Good
Friday and Easter, they have three great annual festivals, partly religious and partly social, when the whole
Society assemble in their large public hall, and relig-
iously feast together. The first of these is the Anni-
versary of the Founding of the Society, on the 15th of
February ; the second is their Harvest Home, in early
autumn ; and the third is their annual Love Feast and
Lord's Supper, which they observe together in the latter part of October. On these occasions they are careful to remember those of their brethren who are too
infirm to meet with the rest, and also the stranger and
sojourner among them, by sending liberal portions of
good things from their well furnished table.

As preparatory to partaking of the holy communion,

they are careful to urge the necessity of reconciling all difficulties which may have arisen among any of the members, so that they may participate in true Christian love and fellowship. This is in accordance with our Saviour's injunction in Matt. 5 : 23, " If thou bring thy gift to the altar," &c. As a part also of their preparation for the communion, they have another usage which approximates the Roman Catholic practice of confession. When any one may have indulged in any gross sin, or have any burden resting upon his conscience, he is urged to make a private confession of it to the religious leader, as well as to God ; believing that without this confession to the priest or (minister) they cannot expect that full forgiveness from God which will bring them true peace of mind. In favor of this practice they urge the salutary operation of it as a relief to the conscience, and a defense against future temptation ; besides being sanctioned by the command, "Confess your faults one to another," &c., and by the power of " binding" and " loosing," given in Matt. 18 : 18. There is less of this confession practiced now than in former years, especially in the time of Father Rapp, whom they profoundly reverenced as God's minister ; and when, being younger and less established in the Christian life, they were more liable to yield to temptation or besetting sins.

In former years they had a pious custom, which is attributed to them in the " Encyclopædia of Religious Knowledge,"* of keeping watch by turns at night, and after crying the hour, adding these or like words : "A

---

*The same article gives them credit for "cultivating the learned languages and professions." This they have never done.

day is past, and a step made nearer our end : our time runs away, and the joys of heaven are our reward." The watchman still pursues his nightly rounds, but always *in silence.* The practice of crying the hours was long since laid aside.

FUNERAL CEREMONIES.—Their funeral ceremonies are simple. The elders and a few of the more intimate friends of the deceased assemble at the house where the body lies, and after a few appropriate remarks they follow the hearse in procession to the orchard, where the grave has been prepared. The plain hexagonal coffin which encloses the remains is laid over the grave as usual, a hymn is sung, a few further remarks are made, the coffin is lowered to its resting place, a few flowers are thrown upon it by each of the bystanders, and the grave is quietly filled.

No board, or stone, or monument of any kind, is placed at the head or foot. Only a little elevation of the earth above the surface, with sometimes a shrub or flower planted on it—the affectionate tribute of some near friend—marks each grave. The resting place of Father Rapp himself is thus undistinguished from those of the brethren and sisters who sleep beside him in lengthening rows beneath the apple trees. A register is kept in which the names of the deceased are recorded, with the date of their departure and a number annexed, which serves to distinguish the grave in its row. They nearly all live to a good old age, few dying under seventy, and many reaching even to four score, or more. None of them seem to dread the approach of death. They believe that all who have been good and faithful members of the Society, and who are not permitted to survive until the Lord's coming, will be raised up to meet him at his glorious appearing. Thus they calmly speak of being carried to the orchard, when their work is done, there to sleep until the resurrection morn.

CONCLUSION.—Their aged and helpless ones, of whom there are always some, are carefully and tenderly nursed. A few have been bed-ridden for twenty or thirty years, and are remarkable examples of patient Christian endurance. There are but few young among them, except those who are apprenticed and not full members; and but few of these ever avail themselves of the privilege of a permanent connection with the Society on attaining their majority. Young Germany has become Young America, and he is not disposed to submit to the want of personal property, personal liberty, and a wife—though compensated by all the advantages which membership in a wealthy association brings. Even the prospect of sharing the spoils, if at any future time the Society should be dissolved and its large possessions distributed among the survivors, does not present sufficient attractions to induce all the younger members to retain their connection. Nothing but the strong religious convictions which brought the original members together, and which were intensified and confirmed by the general religious revival which preceded their adoption of the system of celibacy, could have so long held them in union. The younger members, with a few exceptions, and the apprentices, do not become fully imbued with the true spirit of the Society, and they are easily induced to go out into the world.

What is to be the end of all this, is a question difficult to answer. They themselves are not disposed to
be communicative on the subject, especially to strangers. Seriously they hope that the great consummation may arrive soon, while some of them are yet
living; but playfully, they may reply to idle questions,
that the State of Pennsylvania will be glad to inherit
their possessions, as a help toward paying off her debts.
It is to be hoped that, ultimately, some great benevolent foundation may be laid, in which they may become, in a measure, their own executors, and may
contribute in the most effectual way for the promotion
of human welfare, and the advancement of that glorious
kingdom of God which they have been so long expecting. They are doubtless not unmindful of the stew-
ardship with which they have been intrusted, and
of the responsibilities it involves. It is for themselves to determine how they may best meet these
responsibilities. Meanwhile, let the writer and reader
of these chapters be mindful each of his own steward-
ship, for neither of them may live to see the *last of the
Harmonists.*

Since the foregoing chapters were written, the following brief semi-
official statement of their views on certain points, by one of the leaders, has come to hand. It is dated August 3, 1861.

" RELIGION.—We understand from the book of Genesis 1 : 26, that
man was created in the image of God, to have dominion over all
the earth, &c.; also, that our first parents, by disobedience, committed
a transgression against the command of God, and fell from that original elevation, and became corrupt and unfit to possess the garden of
Eden, which was intended for their abode. God passed sentence, and
expelled them from Eden, into this world which we now inhabit. In
this corrupt state man has invented a vast deal of good, which is evidence of his original greatness; he has also revealed and brought
into action a vast deal of evil: those two facts cannot be denied

They constitute two central points, which are represented by the Word of God—Jesus Christ on the one side, and the Angel of darkness on the other. The latter was the instigator and the beginning of all evil, but shall have his head bruised by the woman's seed. Gen. 3 : 15. Jesus Christ is the woman's seed who has bruised that head and will continue to bruise it by his followers in time and eternity, until the influence of evil is entirely cut off and subdued through Jesus Christ and his people, and ultimately God be God in all. Cor. 15 : 27-28. Religion, therefore, is the medium to raise fallen man up to his former dignity. The doctrine of Christ and his apostles is the true religion. If this is rightly understood, believed, and put into practice in spirit and in truth, by thoughts, words and acts, it will work a full *regeneration* and produce a new man, or the image of God, through Jesus Christ, to love God above all, and man as ourselves. In this lies the fulfilment of law and gospel."

To this may be added the following old memorandum of some of Mr. Rapp's doctrines, by one who was not a member, but which is admitted to be correct :

"Mr. Rapp taught, 1st. A doctrine of future rewards and punishments. 2d. Did not teach the doctrine of everlasting punishment. 3d. Taught that the end of the world was nigh, it might be to-morrow; but he varied the time, extending it sometimes to 1837. 4th. Taught that there must not be carnal intercourse between man and woman, married or unmarried. 5th. That such only as refrained from such intercourse would inherit the brightest places, or most perfect happiness in the other world."

For a further exhibition of religious views kindred with those of the Harmonists, see Appendix F.

APPENDIX A.

"CHILIASTIC DREAMS." (See Introduction, p. 17.)

" About the close of the 10th century, a very wild and extraordinary delusion arose and spread itself, and at length so far prevailed as not only to subdue the reason, but to actuate the conduct of multitudes. It proceeded from a misinterpretation of the well known passage in the Revelation, ch. 20, 'And he laid hold of the dragon, that old serpent, which is the devil and Satan, and bound him a *thousand years*,' &c. It does not appear that the earlier divines derived from this prophecy that specific expectation respecting the moment of the world's dissolution, which now became general, nor do we learn that the people before this time, much busied themselves about a matter which could not possibly affect their own generation (it being the prevailing tradition among commentators, that the period of 'a thousand years' commenced with the manifestation, or the passion of Christ, and that the establishment of the Christian church was to be regarded as the 'first resurrection' and the first epoch of the period of a thousand years'); but about the year 960, as the season approached nearer, one Bernhard, a hermit of Thuringia, a person not destitute of knowledge, boldly promulgated (on the faith of a particular revelation from God) the certain assurance, that at the end of the thousandth year, the fetters of Satan were to be broken, and after the reign of Antichrist should be terminated, that the world would be consumed by sudden conflagration. There was something plausible in the doctrine, and it was peculiarly suited to the gloomy superstition of the age: the clergy adopted it without delay; the pulpits loudly resounded with it; it was diffused in every direction with astonishing rapidity, and embraced with an ardor proportioned to the obscurity of the subject, and the greediness of human credulity. The belief pervaded and possessed every rank of society, not as a cold and indifferent assent, but as a motive for the most important undertakings. Not nobles only, but princes, and even bishops, are mentioned as having made pilgrimages to Palestine on this occasion. Many abandoned their friends and their families, and hastened to the shores of Palestine, with the pious persuasion that Mount Sion would be the throne of Christ, when he should descend to judge the world; and these, in order to secure a more partial sentence from the God of mercy and charity, usually made over their property before they departed, to some adjacent church or monastery; others whose pecuniary means were thought, perhaps, insufficient to bribe the justice of Heaven, devoted thier personal service to the same establishments, serving in the character of slaves, and hoping that the supreme Judge would be more favorable to them, if they made themselves servants to his servants. In many places, edifices both sacred and secular were suffered to go to decay, and in some instances actually pulled down, from the expectation that they would be no longer needed. Whenever an eclipse of the sun or moon took place, most persons betook themselves to the shelter of rocks and caverns, as if the temples of nature were destined to preservation amidst the wreck of man and his works. Almost all the donations which were made to the church in this century, were prefaced with the words, ' *Appropinquante mundi termino,*' &c. (*i. e. the end of the world being now at hand*). This general delusion was opposed, indeed, by a few wiser individuals, but nothing could overcome it, till the century had closed. But when the century ended without any great calamity, the greater part began to understand that John had not really predicted what they so much feared.''—*Mosheim's and Waddington's Church History.*

The *Crusades* also, those wild and fanatical expeditions to the Holy Land during the middle ages, were the fruit, in part, of these '' Chiliastic dreams.'' The habit of making pilgrimages to Palestine, which is mentioned above, continued to prevail even after the close of the 10th century. Great merit was supposed to be acquired by these pilgrimages, and the reports which the returning pilgrims brought respecting the wrongs and cruelties inflicted upon them by the Moslems who held the Holy Sepulchre, fired the hearts of those thousands who set forth for the rescue of the holy places from infidel hands.

Meanwhile the millennarian interpreters continued to reconstruct their Chiliastic schemes, and to keep up the prevailing delusion that the throne of the Messiah was soon to be set up on Mount Sion, and that all true pilgrims and Crusaders would share in the honors of his kingdom.

Again, at the time of the Reformation in the 16th century, the *Anabaptists* arose, and, by their '' Chiliastic dreams'' and other fanatical follies, brought great reproach upon the more sober millennarian views of Luther and the other reformers. They were a turbulent and seditious people, who " repudiated all human laws and magistrates, and set themselves to subvert all existing institutions, in order to realize the kingdom of their dreams. Instead of leaving to Christ to establish his own kingdom in his own time and way, they undertook to establish it with fire and sword, and took a certain tailor, John Buckholdt, and set him up as " King of Zion," in the name and place of Jesus, regarding him as the representative of God himself, the Lord of all the earth, by whose administration all worldly powers were to be rooted up, the wicked exterminated, a kingdom of saints established in this world, without having to wait the time of the " resurrection of the just." (Seiss.) They taught the people to despise their lawful rulers, and the salutary regulations by which all communities exist. Everywhere it was the cry of these enthusiastic visionaries, " no tribute, all things in common, no tithes, no magistrates, the baptism of infants is an invention of the devil," &c. (Milner.) Bimiler and his followers (referred to in the Introduction, p. 19,) seem to have entertained kindred views.

The *Millerites*, of our own country, are also in the recollection of all, as being a class of Chiliastic dreamers, who ventured to fix the precise day of the Lord's coming; first, in the month of April, 1842, and then, on the 22d of October, 1843. Thousands of our countrymen, and not a few in Great Britain, embraced these notions, and many had prepared their "ascension robes," and were gathered together in various places, in confident expectation that the Lord would then appear.

About twelve years ago, the sect of Adventists had again, as they supposed, discovered the precise day, and many of them sat all day in their houses in solemn expectation of the great event.

APPENDIX B.

COLONY TO RUSSIAN TARTARY.

(See Introduction, p. 18.)

Extract from Blumhardt's "Handbuchlein der Missionsgeschichte," p. 153, 161–2.

" In the years 1817–1819, about five hundred German families, mostly from Würtemberg, emigrated to and settled in (Asiatic) Georgia, under the auspices of the Russian Government. The chief motives or cause of their emigration were, partly, liturgical changes in the church of their native land, and partly, the hope of the speedy return of the Lord —an occasion on which they deemed it desirable to be near the Holy Land.   In the region of the river Kur they founded seven colonies ; which, however, to their own injury and against the express advice of the Czar, were placed at a distance of about eighty leagues from one another.   They are called New Tiflis, Alexandersdorf, Marienfeld, with Petersdorf, Elisabethal, Katharinenfeld, Annenfeld, Helenendorf. They received perfect freedom of religion and worship along with other privileges, and they chose their spiritual superiors or directors from among themselves.   Most of them had brought with them from home a considerable store of Christian knowledge, and much active Christian life was manifest among them.   However their hopes were not realized.   In the midst of strange and half savage people and customs, their economical relations did not long continue in a favorable condition.   During the war between Russia and Persia, in 1826, they had the misfortune of being exposed to the incursions of robber hordes from the Turkish and Persian borders.   Most of them were compelled to flee for their lives, leaving all they had to become the prey of the plunderers.   Many were dragged away as slaves.   Katharinenfeld was entirely destroyed, and only the speedy victory of the Russians rescued the settlements from utter desolation. Not less injurious were the controversies which, from the first, they carried on with one another, as in every village, especially in Katharinenfeld, there were two parties hotly opposed to each other on matters of faith or doctrine.

In 1822, several German missionaries, the first fruits of the mission school at Basel, settled in Astrachan—not with the view of remaining there permanently, but to learn the languages of the East, and at their leisure to select a place for their future labors.   Here they were soon convinced that direct and immediate efforts for the conversion of the Mussulmans would be untimely (the Christian name was so utterly despised), and that they must proceed modestly and quietly in the way of preparation for future efforts.   This preparation they hoped to effect in three ways : 1. By labors among the scattered colonists. 2. By a revival of the ancient churches. 3. By the diffusion of books and tracts adapted to the awakening of the Mohammedans.   The carrying out of the first of these plans obviously led them to Georgia (or Grusien), to their own countrymen of the colonies on the river Kur.   The Basel missionaries were very actively employed among these people.   They also introduced a new spiritual ritual or church-service, founded on the Augsburg Confession, which received the imperial sanction (the Czar's). Then in 1824 Saltet was appointed (and recognized by the government) as an itinerant preacher ; and as the government assured to each local preacher a salary of one thousand rubles, all the villages were by degrees provided with pastors from Basel, who were under the supreme direction of Saltet, as rector or chief pastor at Tiflis. Saltet died of cholera in 1830, and his place was filled next by August Dittrich, and then by Bonwetch. However welcome this spiritual care and superintendence were to the colonists at first, the preachers, after all, received small thanks for their self-sacrificing toils ; a separatist spirit showed itself ever more and more decided in opposition to all church order and dicipline. The labor expended upon these communities has consequently had no special significance or results in regard to the mission work."

THE ZOARITES. (See Introduction, p. 19.)

Extract from Emil Klauprecht's " Deutsche Chronik in der geschichte der Ohio-Thales," p. 167.

" Similar to Rapp's settlement was that of the Zoarites in Tuscarawas county, Ohio. It also shows how simply and naturally German peasants and weavers fall into communism, and how intelligently they can carry out the system. As in other instances, so also in the case of these people, religious caprice or independence, in the old Swabian villages, came into conflict with the government, and therefore in the spring of 1817 they left their native land, about one hundred and fifty in number, and reached Philadelphia in August. Joseph Bäumler (Bimiler), a young man, had during the voyage, by his mild and prudent conduct and behavior, gained the confidence of his companions. He had been first a weaver and then a teacher, and now his uncommon talent for organization became manifest. Certain Quakers of Philadelphia sold to the Society at a fair price and on a long credit, five thousand six hundred acres of land, formerly military land, lying around old Fort Laurens, in Tuscarawas county, Ohio. They arrived at the place in the winter. They were poor, destitute of all means to render life even in some measure tolerable; cattle, farming utensils, and furniture, were equally wanting. They first sought shelter in the most wretched huts ; they had to suffer from hunger, cold, and wet; fever committed great devastation among them, but their religious communion and fellowship

held them together. After they had kept house individually or by families, for more than a year, they deemed it
better to unite themselves into a community of property
and industry, in order more effectually by associated labor
to overcome the difficulties with which they had to contend.
The cholera of the year 1832 produced fearful ravages among
them; fifty members of the community fell its victims.
From that time, however, their property increased with
every year. Their property amounted to considerably more
than a million of dollars; they possessed nine thousand acres
of land in one tract, most excellent herds of cattle, an oil
mill, a saw mill, a flour mill, two smithies, and a cloth
manufactory. They carried on a considerable trade with
their productions, and had profitable sums of money deposited in bank.''

THE GERMAN SETTLERS IN EASTERN PENN-SYLVANIA.

It is further worthy of remark that most of the earlier
German emigration to Eastern Pennsylvania, originated
in a desire to escape from religious disabilities and persecutions. During the religious troubles in Germany in the
beginning of the 17th century, the French Catholics threatened to devastate the whole Protestant country of the
Rhine provinces and elsewhere, in which attempt they partially succeeded. At this time, and subsequently, many respectable and opulent farmers left their homes for North
America, and settled mostly in Eastern Pennsylvania. William Penn himself had visited Germany, and had traveled
and preached there extensively in 1677, five years before the
date of the royal charter for the colony of Pennsylvania.
Besides those who embraced his peculiar views, there were
great numbers of other religious people, who availed themselves of the opportunity of emigrating to a colony which
was under the administration of so benign a governor.

In 1742 the number of these early emigrants and their
children amounted to one hundred thousand souls. Many
also settled in New York, South Carolina and Georgia, but
did not prosper as well as those in Pennsylvania.

The prevalence of various minor German sects in Eastern
Pennsylvania, such as Moravians, Mennonites, Dunkers,
Ummish, &c., is the result of these early emigrations.
They were not only a religious people, but were the model
farmers of the country. Thus it will be seen that Germany
as well as Great Britain, Ireland, and France, sent its '' Pilgrim Fathers'' to this country.

APPENDIX C.

ANCIENT COMMUNISTS. (See p. 98.)

THE history of socialism from the earliest times, would be an interesting and instructive one; but the writer has not the authorities at hand to enable him to give even a brief sketch of the various attempts which have been made toward such a reorganization of human society. It is well known, however, that all such attempts have been on a very limited scale, and of comparatively short duration. Two examples belonging to ancient times may be noticed as being less known than those more modern.

I. PYTHAGORAS, an old Greek philosopher of the fifth century before Christ, was a practical communist. He taught the doctrine of a celestial harmony, and that there is a certain "music of the spheres" produced by the impulse of the planets upon the ether through which they move; the seven planets producing sounds corresponding with the seven notes of the musical scale. It was a leading thought with him, that the state and the individual ought each in its way, to reflect the image of that order and harmony by which he believed the universe to be sustained and regulated. After having acquired great fame in his own country as a philosopher (a name which he was the first to apply to himself as a *lover of wisdom*), he removed to Crotona, in Southern Italy (Magna Græcia), where he instituted a school for the instruction of young men of the noblest families, in mathematics, politics, and the various branches of science known by the comprehensive name of philosophy. The number of his pupils was at first confined to three hundred, and they formed a society which was at once "a philosophical school, a religious brotherhood, and a political association." We read that, afterward, "The brethren of the Pythagorean college at Crotona, were about six hundred in number, and lived together as in one family with their wives and children, in a public building called ὁμακόϊον or the common auditory. The whole business of the society was conducted with the most perfect regularity. Every day was begun with a distinct deliberation upon the manner in which it should be spent, and concluded with a careful retrospect of the events which had occurred, and the business which had been transacted. They rose before the sun, that they might pay him homage; after which they repeated select verses from Homer, and other poets, and made use of music, both vocal and instrumental, to enliven their spirits and fit

them for the duties of the day. They then employed several hours in the study of science. These were succeeded by
an interval of leisure, which was commonly spent in a soli-
tary walk for the purpose of contemplation. The next portion of the day was allotted to conversation. The hour
immediately before dinner was filled up with various kinds
of athletic exercises. Their dinner (δεῖπνον) consisted chiefly of bread, honey, and water; for after they were perfectly
initiated they wholly abstained from wine. The remainder
of the day was devoted to civil and domestic affairs, conversation, bathing, and religious ceremonies."

Before any one could be admitted into this fraternity, he
had to undergo the severest scrutiny as to his features and
personal appearance; his past conduct toward his parents
and friends, the passions he was most inclined to indulge,
the character of his associates, what incidents excited in him
the strongest emotions of joy or sorrow, &c. Upon the first
admission, which was but probationary, the fortitude of the
candidate was put to a severe trial by a long course of abstinence and silence. He was not permitted to see the master, or to hear his lectures, but from behind a curtain, and
more commonly he was taught the doctrines of Pythagoras
by a more advanced and fully initiated pupil, who was allowed to give no explanations to any inquiries, but silenced
all questionings, by the oracular "*ipse dixit*" of the master. If any one, through impatience of this rigid discipline,
chose to withdraw from the society before the expiration of
his terms of probation, he was dismissed with a share of the
common stock, the *double* of that which he had advanced,
and a tomb was erected for him as for a dead man. (See
Thirlwall and Ritter.)

II. THE ESSENES were a sect of Jewish communists at
the time of our Saviour, and are usually mentioned in connection with the Pharisees and Sadducees of the New Testament. The singular fact that they never came in for a share
of the rebukes which the other Jewish sects received from
Christ and his apostles, and are not even referred to at all in
the New Testament, is accounted for from the circumstance
that they were a sort of *pietistic separatists*, who mingled
but little with other Jews, lived a quiet and secluded life,
did not go up to the three great annual feasts, and yet were
remarkable for their piety toward God; and thus they did
not come in contact with our Saviour, and did not deserve
his reproofs. Neander, in contrasting them with the formalist-
Pharisees, and the skeptical Sadducees, characterizes the
Essenes as "those more quiet but more warm-hearted spirits,

with whom the power of religious feeling or imagination is too predominant, who withdraw into themselves from the strife of the learned in Scripture, and seeking the interpretation of the meaning of the old documents of religion in their subjective feelings or imaginations, become *mystics*, sometimes of a practical, sometimes of a contemplative character." He speaks of them further as " a company of pious men, much experienced in the trials of outward and of the inward life, who had withdrawn themselves out of the strife of theological and political parties, to the western side of the Dead Sea, where they lived together in intimate connection, partly in the same sort of society as the monks of later days, and partly as mystical orders in all periods have done." From this first society, other smaller ones afterward proceeded, and spread themselves over all Palestine. Josephus says, "They have all things in common, so that a rich man enjoys no more of his wealth than he who has nothing ; for it is a law among them, that those who come to them must let what they have be common to the whole order, and so there is as it were, one patrimony among all the brethren. There are about four thousand men that live in this way, and neither marry wives, nor are desirous to keep servants, as thinking the latter tempts men to be unjust, and the former gives the handle to domestic quarrels ; but as they live by themselves they minister to one another. They also have stewards appointed to take care of their common affairs, who have no separate business for any, but what is for the use of them all." " Nor is there ever any clamor or disturbance in their houses, but they give every one leave to speak in their turn, which silence thus kept in their houses appears to foreigners like some tremendous mystery ; the cause of which is, the perpetual sobriety which they exercise, and the same settled measure of meat and drink that is allotted to them and that such as is abundantly sufficient for them." " They do nothing but according to the injunctions of their curators, except to assist those that are in want, and to show mercy ; this they may do of their own accord, but they cannot give anything to their kindred without permission from the curators." " They are eminent for fidelity, and are the ministers of peace : whatsoever they say also is firmer than an oath, but swearing is avoided by them, for they say that he that cannot be believed without swearing is already condemned." " If any one has a mind to come over to their sect, he is not immediately admitted, but he is prescribed the same method of living which they use, for a year, during which he is excluded. Having approved himself during that time as being able to endure their continence, he receives the waters of purification (baptism), and after a trial of two more years he is finally admitted to full fellowship." "After the time of their preparatory trial is over, they are divided into four classes, &c. They are long-lived also, insomuch that many of them live above one hundred years, by means of the simplicity of their diet and their regular course of life. As for death, if it will be for their glory, they esteem it better than living always. When tortured, burnt, and torn to pieces for their religion, they smiled in their very pains, and laughed to scorn those who inflicted the torments, and resigned up their souls with great alacrity, as expecting to receive them again." "Another order of them, who agree with the rest as to their way of living, and customs and laws, differ in the matter of marriage, thinking that if all men were of the same opinion, the whole race of mankind would fail. But they do not marry or have intercourse for the sake of pleasure, but only for the sake of offspring."

They looked upon the law of Moses as an *allegorical* system of spiritual and mysterious truths, and renounced in its explication the literal sense of the Mosaic law; but those who inhabited the deserts of Egypt maintained that *no* sacrifice should be presented to God, except that of a composed mind absorbed in the contemplation of things divine. They observed the Sabbath more carefully than other Jews, not even kindling a fire on that day. They employed themselves in the arts of peace, agriculture, pasturage, handicraft works, and especially in the art of healing, while they took great delight in investigating the healing powers of nature.

The very remarkable resemblance between the notions and practices above described, and those of the Harmonists, Zoarites, and especially of the Shakers (except the dancing), must strike every reader. And yet none of these sects had probably any knowledge of the Essenes. Whence then this striking similarity? It is to be attributed partly, no doubt, to a desire on the part of these modern sects to imitate the primitive Christians, who themselves may have had the example of their Essenite Jewish neighbors before them, in the matter of community of goods; and partly also to the influence of political circumstances, and of a mystical style of religious and philosophical thought which prevailed alike among Essenite Jews and Pietistic Germans.

APPENDIX D.

ARTICLES OF ASSOCIATION. (See pp. 53 and 91.)

WHEREAS, by the favor of Divine Providence, an association or community has been formed by George Rapp and many others, upon the basis of Christian fellowship, the principles of which, being faithfully derived from the sacred Scriptures, include the government of the patriarchal age, united to the community of property, adopted in the days of the apostles, and wherein the simple object sought, is to approximate, so far as human imperfections may allow, to the fulfilment of the will of God, by the exercise of those affections, and the practice of those virtues which are essential to the happiness of man in time and throughout eternity;

And whereas, it is necessary to the good order and well being of the said association, that the conditions of membership should be clearly understood, and that the rights, privileges and duties of every individual therein should be so defined as to prevent mistake or disappointment on the one hand, and contention or disagreement on the other;

Therefore, be it known to all whom it may concern, that we, the undersigned, citizens of the county of Beaver, in the Commonwealth of Pennsylvania, do severally and distinctly, each for himself, covenant, grant and agree, to and with the said George Rapp, and his associates, as follows, viz. :

ARTICLE 1st.   We, the undersigned, for ourselves, our heirs, executors and administrators, do hereby give, grant, and forever convey to the said George Rapp and his associates, and to their heirs and assigns, all our property, real, personal and mixed, whether it be lands and tenements, goods and chattels, money or debts due to us, jointly or severally in possession, in remainder, or in reversion or expectancy, whatsoever and wheresoever, without evasion qualification or reserve, as a free gift or donation, for the benefit and use of the said association, or community, and we do hereby bind ourselves, our heirs, executors and administrators, to do all such other acts as may be necessary to vest a perfect title to the same in the said association, and to place the said property at the full disposal of the superintendent of the said community without delay.

ARTICLE 2d.   We do further covenant and agree to and with the said George Rapp and his associates, that we will severally submit faithfully to the laws and regulations of said community, and will at all times manifest a ready and cheerful obedience toward those who are or may be appointed as superintendents thereof, holding ourselves bound to promote the interest and welfare of the said community, not only by the labor of our own hands, but also by that of our children, our families, and all others who now are, or hereafter may be, under our control.

ARTICLE 3d. If contrary to our expectation it should so happen that we could not render the faithful obedience aforesaid, and should be induced from that, or any other cause, to withdraw from the said association, then and in such case we do expressly covenant and agree to and with the said George Rapp and his associates, that we never will claim or demand, either for ourselves, our children, or for any one belonging to us, directly or indirectly, any compensation, wages or reward whatever for our or their labor or services rendered to the said community, or to any member thereof, but whatever we or our families jointly or severally shall or may do, all shall be held and considered as a voluntary service for our brethren.

ARTICLE 4th. In consideration of the premises, the said George Rapp and his associates do, by these presents, adopt the undersigned jointly and severally, as members of the said community, whereby each of them obtains the privilege of being present at every religious meeting, and of receiving not only for themselves but also for their children and families, all such instructions in church and school, as may be reasonably required, both for their temporal good, and for their eternal felicity.

ARTICLE 5th. The said George Rapp and his associates further agree to supply the undersigned severally with all the necessaries of life, as clothing, meat, drink, lodging, &c., for themselves and their families. And this provision is not limited to their days of health and strength; but when any of them shall become sick, infirm, or otherwise unfit for labor, the same support and maintenance shall be allowed as before, together with such medicine, care, attendance, and consolation, as their situation may reasonably demand. And if at any time after they have become members of the association, the father or mother of a family should die or be otherwise separated from the community, and should leave their family behind, such family shall not be left orphans or destitute, but shall partake of the same rights and maintenance as before, so long as they remain in the association, as well in sickness as in health, and to such extent as their circumstances may require.

ARTICLE 6th. And if it should so happen as above mentioned, that any of the undersigned should violate his or their agreement, and would or could not submit to the laws and regulations of the church or the community, and for that or any other cause should withdraw from the association, then the said George Rapp and his associates agree to refund to him or them, the value of all such property as he or they may have brought into the community, in compliance with the first article of this agreement, the said value to be refunded without interest, in one, two, or three annual instalments, as the said George Rapp and his associates shall determine. And if the person or persons so withdrawing themselves were poor, and brought nothing into the community, notwithstanding they depart openly and regularly, they shall receive a donation in money, according to the length of their stay, and to their conduct, and to such amount as their necessities may require, in the judgment of the superintendents of the association.

In witness whereof, and in testimony that the undersigned have become members of the said community upon the conditions aforesaid, they have hereunto severally and each for himself, set their hands and seals, on the ninth day of March, in the year of our Lord one thousand eight hundred and twenty-seven.

In presence of John H. Hopkins
and Charles S. Voltz.

On the death of George Rapp, 7th of August, 1847, the whole Society signed the above agreement again, putting in two Trustees, and seven Elders, to manage and regulate all matters as George Rapp had done.

APPENDIX E.

EXTRACTS FROM GÖNTGEN'S LETTER, INTRODUCTORY TO THE VISIT OF COUNT LEON.

(See page 72.)

Note—The translation has been made literally, and fitly represents the long, involved, and word-crowded sentences of the original German. We give it with all its verbiage.

Peace, grace, and mercy, as also salvation and blessing, be to the aged Patriarch George Rapp and his associated superintendents, and also to the whole in-God-united-Society of Harmony.

In the quarter of a century which has passed away since you withdrew from the pressure upon freedom of conscience in monarchical Europe, to seek refuge in the free States of North America for the undisturbed realization of your philanthropic ideas and the development of your generally benevolent inclinations, the measure of iniquity in Europe has at last become full! The spiritual order neglected even more and more its appointed end, and became even more and more estranged from the Divine Grace, through striving after external honor and profits, so that the clergy, with very rare exceptions, became utterly unqualified to be instruments to promote the true eternal welfare of believing Christians or children of God. The secular rulers, both high and low, have violently taken to themselves the lordship of God over the bodies and souls of their subjects, so that, instead of administering the divine laws, as the representatives of the Creator, for the advancement of the external and internal prosperity of men, for whom the living Son of God, Jesus Christ, poured out his blood, and over whom as over them too (the rulers), he acquired an unlimited right of property as the King of kings, and instead of protecting the church in the enjoyment of her divine rights, they commit whoredom with the divine word and the divine authority, as they strive after the enjoyment of that honor which belongs to the majesty of God alone: expend the property of the citizens upon worthless or trifling objects, and interfere with and violently oppress all the simple, Christian, peacefulpeople in the land. The people are scourged by their rulers with two-fold rods : *nationally*, by exorbitant taxes and cruel custom-regulations, whereby trade and industry are ruined, and all business brought to a standstill ; *spiritually*, by the suppression and prevention of all exhortations and warnings in regard to amendment. Ignominy and imprisonment are the portion of the clergy and other believers who publicly recognize the holy commandments of the religion of Christ and endeavor honestly to follow them.

At this moment, individually and generally, the despotism of the rulers is becoming intolerable. Laws are abused by their executors in favor of rogues, and administered to the injury of the retired peaceful pious people of the land. This is the experience of thousands, whether in comfortable circumstances or poor, so that the better people are contending with real despair for conscience sake. On account of the blindness of the faithful and the obduracy of the world, no one regarding either the promises or the threats of God, the great day of God's wrath has come, and God will hold judgment upon all flesh that is upon earth. The harvest is ripe, and the fruit of Christ's people is dry, and God will

root from the earth and from his Christian children everything that is ungodly, and all those whose names are not
written in the Lamb's book of life. Therefore, to the angels
and powers of heaven and all elements is the command
given, to pour out the seven vials of the fierce anger of God
over all those in Europe who do not repent and turn with
the whole heart to God. The irrevocable final judgment of
God is pronounced in regard to all men. In Europe fearful
signs, prognostics of the great day of the Lord, are appearing before the near real coming of the Son of man, who will
judge without respect of person, the whole world, according
to their works.

Therefore, by the authority and in the name of the living
God, *an official writing* is addressed to all those in whose
hearts the love of God and faith in the living Triune are
not quite extinct; and it is placed in the hands of the most
important monarchs of Europe, and is especially directed
to the chief shepherds of the Catholic church and to the
enlightened rulers of the other Christian confessions; who
are enjoined, on their everlasting responsibility, to make the
said writing everywhere known to the faithful, and where
possible, to have it printed, that all who read or hear it and
are still susceptible of the divine grace, may be able to re-
form and return with childlike trust to God their Lord.
There is no more time, as God the Lord has already spoken
his judgment upon the whole earth.

The good, true, believers would perish with the ungodly if
God did not take care of his children, in whom all good is nearly extinct. Happy they who shall be found watching in the
fear, faith, and love of God, with lamps full of the oil of good
works! God will gather together these his sheep scattered
through all the world and lead them to a place where they
shall be kept until, &c., &c.

North America is the wilderness where the church exists,
not at all according to the strict external hierarchical connections and relations. All ecclesiastical forms, even the
narrowest and most one-sided sects, all stand side by side
and equally enjoy the protection of the government. Even
atheism is tolerated and permitted, &c. But while the
divine is there pushed into the background, the more freedom is allowed to the humane to develop itself. Hence
the greater receptivity of the North Americans for the
regeneration of Christianity, which finds difficult entrance
among men brought up as they are in Europe, amidst
empty church formalities and the dead letter. While in
America the church is permitted to extend herself with

out limitation or condition, according to the established laws of freedom; in Europe, on the contrary, a man is not allowed to perform the duties he owes as an individual to other men, much less to God. Therefore, the first fruits of the new church of Christ shall be rescued from Europe, and united with all those in America who are prepared of God to be incorporated with the true living Christian congregation. For the Lord has designated America and his *ambassador* in the prediction of the prophet (4 Esdras 12 : 34), "My remaining people will he redeem with mercy, namely, those who escaped to my most outer borders." The first place where the Lord will reveal his divine grace, is *your* Christian Society of Harmony, which is all along distinguished of God by wonderful preservation and increase.

America, which has already contemplated with astonishment this remarkable blessed little people, will be thrown into the greatest amazement, when from this little point the word of divine truth and the fullness of divine blessing, shall be spread abroad over all America.

The Lord has delivered you precisely in the time wherein the type of the anti-christ in France has obtained the highest power and dignity, in order to become the scourge of the nations. Your community has had frequently to change its place of abode, even in the free States, in order that those might be separated from it who could not sincerely and with the whole heart attach themselves to such a purely humane union, until you have now arrived at the resting place, where the Lord will visit you all with his grace.

It was an omen or token from God, that you should build a church in the form of a cross, in accordance with a vision in sleep, and that you chose the "golden rose"* for the symbol, according to the prophet Micah; for this golden rose shall in truth come to you; yea, the divine Holy Ghost which proceeds from the Father and the Son shall make his abode with you. *You*, in a truly humane, religious spirit, founded a colony whose constitution was grounded upon the words in the Acts of the Apostles : "And the multitude of the faithful were of one heart, &c., and no one said of his goods that they were his own, but all things were in common," so that you have united yourselves on

---

* Allusion is here made to Luther's version of Micah 4 : 8, "Unto thee shall come the golden rose, the first dominion," &c. The church built by the Society on the Wabash was in the form of a cross, having emblazoned above its front entrance a large gilded rose, in accordance with a vision or dream of Father Rapp.

the common principles—love to God and good will toward men, purity of life, and community of goods. Therefore, your fame has resounded in all lands, that the members of your community with the greatest joy frequent the religious assemblies, and that the moral conduct of the community is blameless, that no vicious customs are found in vogue, no cursing or swearing heard, no extravagance seen; that to cheating there is no temptation, because no individual needs money or fears want; that you present a singular example in that you abstain [?] from using the intoxicating drinks which you manufacture as a branch of industry; yea, that of free will you have laid upon yourselves abstinence from sexual intercourse, &c. Through the internal arrangement and external organization of your community, God has declared himself for the preparation for the future, when he will " reveal himself to the little, and will bring to shame those mighty in their own esteem."

Therefore, he hath shown in a living example what man on a human stand-point, in faith and trust in his Creator, is able to achieve for the general good of his fellow men, and has made your town the type of the kingdom of God. Just as even individual details in your Society are carried out simply according to the will of God, so will the Lord reveal himself to you in the general also—and according to his divine law will establish himself in your community, through and in which he has laid the first foundation-stone of the city of God in truth, in order to prepare the future constitution of his Divine Kingdom, and by degrees to bring into connection with you all who are called to eternal life. Then all those who hunger and thirst after righteousness will be fed *gratis* with the bread of eternal life, and given to drink the living waters of divine grace, while on the other hand, all the ungodly shall be rooted out and cast into eternal fire.

Since now God will not suffer his human children to pine in wretchedness of body and soul, and fall into eternal ruin, now the eternal decrees shall be fulfilled, and no human power on earth shall be able to hinder the decreed and outspoken will of God, and to frustrate the work of divine righteousness. Therefore, it is also impossible for THE ANOINTED AND SENT OF GOD to direct and turn things according to human views and wishes, or according to political hopes and expectations, or otherwise than as the express law of God exacts and orders.

The elucidation of the divine will in verity in the generally known *writing* attests and legitimates (as has been imparted to all the mighty ones of Europe), for all and every one, at once, the *contents* of the same as purely divine, as well as *him* through whom therein God reveals his will, as a true plenipotentiary of God. According to the prediction of the prophet (Zech. 4 : 14), he is shown forth, and he will justify himself by the fulfilment of the divine mysteries —that to the *descendant of David* is given the power of the keys of David, or the power to bind and to loose, as also to judge and to decide according to justice and righteousness.

The Anointed of God, from the stem of Judah, of the root of David, who as man has passed through all the trials, physical and spiritual, of life, and hath endured, according to the example of Christ, every indignity and persecution from officials and people of all classes, hitherto however in silence like a sheep that is led to slaughter; he knows and loudly confesses before God and all the world, that he is the least and smallest, but also that there is nothing to him more sacred than the honor of God, &c.

Before the elect children of God, rescued through flight, shall have reached your neighborhood, you will probably have heard of the terrible judgments of God which have already commenced in Europe, and which will extend farther—shortly before and simultaneously with the flight-journey of the little Philadelphian community* of God— who, on their arrival in America, look forward to a christian brotherly reception from you, through the grace of God, and expect philanthropic support. At the same time you have no cause to be anxious that the care for their maintenance will burden you alone, for the Christian strangers carry with them what it was possible to rescue (of their goods), and are, besides, rich through the spiritual treasure of Christian hope, in the living conviction that *there* will be

---

* The *Philadelphian Society* was the name which Count Leon gave to his community at Phillipsburg (see p. 78); and it is probable that he borrowed this name from that of a society which was founded under the same name in 1697, by one Jane Leade, who spent most of her life in reading the works of Jacob Bohm, and penning down her own revelations, &c. Her writings, published at her own expense, are said to fill eight volumes. She had many followers. The name *Philadelphian* (*i. e.*, brotherly love,) was adopted because she believed that all contentions among Christians would cease, provided all would commit their souls to the *internal teacher,* to be moulded, enlightened and governed by him, neglecting all other doctrines, precepts and opinions. She believed that her Philadelphian Society was the very Church of Christ, in which alone the Holy Spirit resided, and that it would supersede all others before the end of the world. She held also the doctrine of the *final restoration* of all things. See Murdoch's Mosheim's Church History, vol. iii., p. 550-1.

fulfilled the promise (Rev. 3 : 7–12), "And to the angel of the church in Philadelphia, write : These things saith he that is holy, he that is true, he that hath the key of David, he that openeth and no man shutteth ; and shutteth, and no man openeth ; I know thy works : behold, I have set before thee an open door, and no man can shut it : for thou hast a little strength, and hast kept my word, and hast not denied my name. Behold, I will make them of the synagogue of Satan, which say they are Jews, and are not, but do lie ; behold, I will make them to come and worship before thy feet, and to know that I have loved thee. Because thou hast kept the word of my patience, I also will keep thee from the hour of temptation, which shall come upon all the world, to try them that dwell upon the earth : Behold, I come quickly: hold that fast which thou hast, that no man take thy crown. Him that overcometh will I make a pillar in the temple of my God, and he shall go no more out : and I will write upon him the name of my God, and the name of the city of my God, which is new Jerusalem, which cometh down out of heaven from my God: and I will write upon him my new name."

In the commission of the *Ambassador and Anointed of God*, of the *Stem of Judah*, of the *Root of David*, written by SAM-UEL, a fellow-servant, and consecrated servant of God, in the profane world now really subsisting Chief Librarian of the free City of Frankfort, Doctor of Philosophy and Theology.

JOHN GEORGE GÖNTGEN.

Frankfort-on-the-Main, July 14, 1829.

APPENDIX F.

THE following extended and characteristic passages have been translated from a small volume, entitled *"Hirten Brief, &c.;* or, Pastoral Letter to true and genuine Free Masons of the ancient system, in the year 5785."

Although the Harmonists are not Free Masons, yet so highly did they esteem this work, that they had it reprinted in 1855, and a copy placed in every family of the Society. It very nearly coincides with their own views. It abounds in sublime conceptions, but the reader will soon find himself carried out into distant nebulous regions of thought, where he will be lost in a fog-cloud of words hard to be understood. It is a fair specimen of the style of thought and language adopted by the theosophic mystics. Its author is unknown, but the speculations are those of Jacob Böhm and his school.

We give entire the introductory remarks which the learned translator has been kind enough to prefix, pertaining to the history of Freemasonry, and the life of Jacob Böhm (or Boehmen, as it is often written).

INTRODUCTORY REMARKS,

BY THE TRANSLATOR.

Every one knows that Freemasonry assumed several different forms or modifications on the continent of Europe, during the early and middle years of the eighteenth century. This is indeed admitted by English and American Masons of "the straitest sect," though they may maintain that "the most ancient and venerable order" was truly represented by not more than one of the many lines of lodges which had by degrees established themselves in France and Germany. In Germany, as in America, the motives which led men to become Freemasons were various. One desired and hoped in this manner to secure for himself in the lodge a respectable place of resort, in which he could always find congenial society. Another was influenced by the view of insuring himself against material want, by an interest in the benevolent and beneficent agencies of an order believed to be wealthy. One aimed at gaining friends, and frustating the power and intrigues of enemies. Another was fascinated and drawn into the order, by its lofty moral and historical claims and pretensions, and by the halo of mysterious and unfathomed antiquity in which its beginnings were believed to be enveloped; and the mere desire to learn "the great secret" was, no doubt, a powerful attraction to many minds. Some may have looked upon the lodge as a debating club, in which they might, by practice, acquire the art of eloquence. Heinrich Steffens, the celebrated physicist and professor, in his autobiography, informs us that the great Prussian Field-Marshal Blücher, who used to astonish and rouse to enthusiasm whole brigades by his oratory, who in fact spoke as well as he fought, "was said to have acquired his remarkable facility of speech at the Freemasons' lodge."

Whatever motives may have prompted persons to become Freemasons, men of different characters and antecedents were accustomed to assign different reasons for remaining in he order and recommending it to others. The mechanic found his trade and calling honored and magnified, when he saw the common life and toils of a hand-worker like himself, invested with antique dignity, and idealized into "something new and strange," "*immensum infinitumque.*" Men of imaginative character, of a cast of mind at once poetical and speculative, were able to discern in the symbols and ceremonies of Freemasonry, the embodiment and practical inculcation of the great principles which lie at the foundation of civilization. Thus Lessing* shows how the order may be the means of bringing into connection and useful co-operation those men of all lands, who are exalted by natural endowments, or acquired culture, or innate sympathies, above the petty and repelling influences of sect, nationality, and traditions; how it may be one of the mightiest agencies for "the education of the human race," while its secret may be nothing more than the conviction that no secret exists to be discovered or revealed.

The Christian theologian, on the other hand, saw in "true and genuine Freemasonry" nothing but Christianity. He was convinced that the chief end of "the holy order" and the chief end of true Christianity were identical; that real Freemasons constituted that sublime and consecrated priesthood, of which the Crucified One was the Head, that they were "brethren of the Cross," and that any man claiming to belong to the mystical fraternity who denied the divinity of Christ, was either an impostor, or he was utterly ignorant of the character which he pretended to sustain. The writer of this letter had in mind a class of nominal Freemasons, who were known to entertain false views on this and kindred subjects. This appears from innumerable passages in the letter; and in the short introduction or preface, the writer says, "Our holy brotherhood has for some time had the misfortune to contain some members who forget what they owe to the Man who has in his hands the fate of the whole order, yea, of the whole human race." "These unhappy persons see not the light at clear midday, partly because the eye is lacking to see with, partly because the medium through which it should ray into the soul is discolored and impure. To supply the former want is not now in our power; for the second, however, we have prepared a remedy, from which we expect the best issue."

The author says he writes not for all the brethren, but for a certain class of them. He has nothing for those who are "full and increased with goods." He writes not for those who have attained perfection, nor for those who, though

* See Lessing's Gesammelte Werke, 2 Band, s. 334, 335.

still on the road, are nearing their great aim—but for the new and inexperienced brethren, who are hungering for truth and illumination. "Utterly profane readers are begged to leave our letter unread, unless they possess the inquiring spirit in a high degree, or unless they have already learned to find the truth worthy of love, in whatever garb it may appear. 'Where I understand the man, he compels my approval. Why then should I not suppose that there is truth where I fail to understand him?' This was the admirably candid and modest judgment of a great man." The writer then adds, that he fears not the criticism of any one who reads his production in this spirit.

"*Jesus is God*—these words constitute our pastoral epistle. The Light of the inner world is the reflection of Jesus, as Jesus is the reflection of the Father of all. The inner world bore the outer world. The affinity between them is therefore close and intimate. The transition from the lower to the upper takes place through mediate substances. The glorified humanity of Jesus is the first of these substances from above downward, as the natural light is the first from below upward. The union of the two, with the enthronement of the Divine Spirit, is the end of regeneration, and this is the way to the treasure of external nature." "In these words," concludes the writer, "you have our plan. Never lose sight of it. This is the guiding thread of Ariadne, which can and must conduct you surely to the goal."

The words quoted above in regard to the connection between the upper and the lower worlds, will remind some readers of the question suggested by the angel in Milton:

> "What if earth
> Be but the shadow of heaven, and things therein
> Each to other like more than on earth is thought?"

And a mystical poet of Persia, in a little poem translated by Tholuck, affirms what is here merely suggested as a question. "The world of sense," says he, "a shadow is of the spirit-world."[*]

We greatly fear, however, that to most readers, the style and teaching of the epistle will appear exceedingly obscure, so nebulous indeed, that we should not be surprised to hear some of them affirm, that the words conveyed no meaning to their minds. In truth, we are compelled in candor to confess—in the words which Cicero employs when thankfully acknowledging the receipt from his friend Atticus of a celebrated Greek-book written by one Serapion—"Hardly

---

[*] See "Trench on the Parables," p. 25.

the thousandth part of it do I understand."* But what of that? Some of the most admirable productions of the human intellect are hard to be understood. The Timæus of Plato is not a luminous dialogue, nor is Hegel's Philosophy always comprehensible at a glance. The latter illustrious philosopher, when dying, lamented that he was leaving behind him on earth only one man capable of expounding his system, and *he*, alas! did not quite understand it.

The "Hirten Brief" belongs to a kind of physico-metaphysical speculation, which for several centuries has had earnest cultivation in Germany. It will be at once recognized, by every one having the slightest knowledge of the subject, as a legitimate product of the mystical school of which Jacob Boehmen was the founder. This remarkable man was born at Altseidenburg, in Upper Lusatia, in the year 1575. His parents were poor country people, whom their son helped in their work by watching the cattle. Even while a mere lad, he used to see strange things in visions of the night, and sometimes of the day: a circumstance which his adherents afterward referred to as evidence of his divine call, and his enemies, as proof of his mendacity. He learned the trade of a shoemaker, and became ultimately a master workman in Görlitz, where he married the daughter of a butcher. After suffering much petty persecution, he died at Görlitz in 1624. From time to time through his whole life he was favored with visions. One of the most remarkable of these he saw in the year 1600, in the twenty-fifth year of his age. "Looking at *a bright tin vessel*, a beautiful, joy-inspiring spectacle, he believed himself to be grasped by a ray of the higher life and hurried away into the centre of mysterious nature."†

We must recollect that the nature of metals played an important part in the system of the mystics, if we would understand how the sight of a tin vessel—which would leave us cool enough—could produce such an effect upon the imagination of Boehmen. The impression of these visions was deepened by intercourse with some physicians who were devoted to the occult sciences, and who by their erudite Paracelsian language exerted much influence upon Boehmen's style of expression. In the year 1610 Boehmen, quite illiterate though he was, felt called upon to appear as an author. His first work bore the following title: "Morning-dawn in the East,

---

* Fecisti mihi pergratum, quod Serapionis librum ad me misisti; ex quo quidem ego (quod inter nos liceat dicere) *millesimam partem vix intelligo.*—Cicero, Epist. ad Att., lib. ii. 4.

† Hagenbach's "Evangel. Protestantismus in seiner geschichtlichen Entwickelung," 1 Band, p. 338, et al.

that is, the Root or Mother of Philosophia, Astrologia, and Theologia," &c., &c. This work was in course of time followed by others, and Jacob Boehmen became widely known. His speculations were received by many as truth, his disciples and admirers multiplied—he was called by them sometimes simply *Philosophus Teutonicus*—the German philosopher, and sometimes the "inspired shoemaker." The number of his opponents and persecutors also increased, and to them he was "The Knight of the Wax," and "the crazy cobbler of Görlitz."* His fame soon extended into foreign lands. We are told by Sir David Brewster, that "Sir Isaac Newton was a diligent student of Jacob Boehmen's writings, and that there were found among his papers copious extracts from them in his own hand-writing." The same writer also says, that it is stated in a letter of Mr. Law (William Law, author of "Call to the Unconverted"), that Charles First was a diligent reader and admirer of Jacob Boehmen, that he sent a well qualified person from England to Görlitz, in Upper Lusatia, to acquire the German language, and to collect every anecdote he could meet with there relative to this great alchemist." We need scarcely add, that "the German philosopher" was believed, among other secrets of nature, to have discovered the art of making gold.

The fame and influence of Boehmen did not die away with the century in which he lived. Among the religious peasantry of his native land, in many an humble farm-house and secluded village, his works, family heir-looms, have been thumbed and pondered over by successive generations, from their first publication until the present time. And not only the obscure and the uninstructed acknowledge his influence and genius. Schelling avowed "affectionate reverence for his labors," and once declared, *ex cathedra*, that "from great Plato down to Master Hegel, no one had appeared worthy to loose the shoe latchet of the profound shoemaker." The great English philosopher, Samuel Taylor Coleridge, says : "My obligations to Boehmen have been direct. I owe him a debt of gratitude."† We must, however, state that these flattering estimates are rather exceptional than otherwise among the judgments of the learned, and that probably a large majority of those who attempt to study Boehmen's works, give a hearty assent to the opinion of Adelung, who assigns him one of the first places in his "History of Human Folly." This fact, however, is not his condemnation; "fit audience, though few," was the desire of one of the greatest

* Hagenbach, *ubi supra.*
† Works, vol. 3, 264, Harper's edition

earthly speakers. And it cannot be denied, that the admirers and disciples of Jacob Boehmen and his school, have, many of them, been remarkable for deep spiritual insight and irreproachable purity of life.

HIRTEN BRIEF;

OR, LETTER TO TRUE AND GENUINE FREE MASONS OF THE ANCIENT SYSTEM.

PART I.

General object of the Letter—Theosophic views of the Trinity and of Creation—The " Seven Spirits," and their office—The Cross the Fountain of all True Light, &c.

The chief end of this letter is to vindicate the Godhead of our most high brother-master (Christ), his identity with the Father, and then the necessity as well as the beneficent consequences of his incarnation. Yes—our object is to elucidate these three great, all-comprehensive subjects, and to impress them upon your hearts, an object of unspeakable dignity, of unutterable importance. Should we succeed, we shall have accomplished all, and shall have the pure heavenly joy of seeing you, weary and heavy laden, come to Jesus, that he may fully kindle the smoking flax and mend again the broken reed.

In order to accomplish our three-fold object, we must show you the entire venerable series or chain of truths, member by member, which comprehends the whole threefold wisdom imparted by God to your fathers from the beginning. God himself not only holds the highest member of this chain, but as being independent, eternal truth, he pervades and animates all, even the most remote links or members of it. Through him they are what they are, viz., sparks, or little drops exactly harmonizing among themselves from the infinite ocean of all truth and goodness. We wish to show you the gradation or scale of these truth-drops, according to the measure of the spirit that impels us—to place in your hands a systematic view of doctrine, in which the deepest didactic and life-truths will present themselves to you, and you will be enabled as it were to touch with the hand the whole connection of the universe. We must, however, go out into the most remote point of the creation, yea, beyond nature and creation; we must ascend to that nameless Being of all beings, whose name consists in that *he is*— we must, in humility and reverence, contemplate what God was before the creation, what he is now, and what he will be through all eternity. From him we descend then into nature and creation; we proceed even to their most extreme limits by the leading string of wisdom. Deeply bowed before him as children in his house, we gaze at the All-Father of the whole, as he makes worlds, causes world to arise from world, peoples them partly with free and partly with mechanical creatures; to the former he is at once father and bridegroom (John 10:30, Mark 2:19), and sows the spaces of immensity with immeasurable systems of suns. Hereupon we come upon that unhappy place of the universe where the Son of the morning forgot that he was a merely finite, limited being, and misused his freedom in the most miserable way. The consequences of this transgression we see become the occasion that God creates a new world, and peoples it with a new race of beings. Adam was the first happy inhabitant of it; but the envy of the rejected Angel plunged him down into the chaos of misery, which he has transmitted even to us.

The state of man before the fall, and then his present state, with what he must become to fulfil his destination; further, the exalted means of his transformation and the blessed consequence of the same—among which are embraced *the treasure of the wise*, yea, the mastery over all nature, &c.—all these things will be revealed to our inquiring eyes.

Let us for a moment, in thought, annihilate all that is created, and we shall then have nothing before us save the infinite, eternal, omnipresent God. Proceed we then in this way farther back, and with an eye full of timid reverence we behold the eternal generation of the Triune—we shall at length in God himself strike upon an unnamable *Somewhat*, to go beyond which is impossible without being lost in a boundless abyss. We would name this inexpressible Somewhat the *Ungrounded* or the *Bottomless*—the eternal, independent One—the unsearchable Deep, which incessantly swallows up all finite understanding. Here we would attach our thread in order to descend into the outermost creation.

This mysterious Unfathomed is a being that produces or bears from himself; all, however, that it bears is God. The primordial will of the Fathomless to bring forth and feel himself, is that which the Holy Scripture calls the *Father* in the Godhead—who is greater than all, while he has in himself the immortal life-principle,—is independent in the highest sense of the word; from him also all fatherhood in heaven and earth proceeds. The pure Begotten of this primordial will is called the *Son*—the perfect image of the Father, the reflection of his majesty, the created light, the first-born before every creature, in whom the Father sees, tastes, and in a divine way enjoys and feels himself; to whom also he has given to have life in himself, and in whom he has his entire, sole, and undivided good pleasure. The Bond between the Father and the Son is the *Holy Ghost*, who constantly goes forth from both, with both is co-essential, and therefore all that he has receives from the Father and the Son, and gives to them again. For what the Father has, the Son also has, and the outflow from both is the Holy Ghost, who brings forth divine life and motion, and bears back again into the paternal abyss all that whatever the divine primordial will has begotten in and out of himself. Out of or beside this Triune Divine Deep, before the creation of finite beings, there was naught. It was this alone that filled all in all, as once again after the ending of the determined æons in created existence, it will also be all in all. It is like an infinite circle, whose centre is every where, whose periphery is nowhere. In this circle place a fiery triangle, and you will have a faint image of the Triune independence, or self-existence, in as far as it is permitted to help forward our imagination by lines and figures.

Love, or a desire of impartation, was the motive which impelled the All-Sufficient to become a creator. To this, passive matter or substratum was necessary, on which to establish the kingdom of the future world of spirits. At this period, however, as already said, beside the Triune in his whole immensity there was naught. He stepped then as it were out of himself, and bore from his innermost being the first foundation for creation (Psalm 33:9). *Divine bringing forth* is called speaking; for when God speaks, or commands, it stands fast. The first thing, however, which God utters, or begets through speaking, is called in the Scripture, *wisdom* (Proverbs 3:19, &c.); and as God can produce from himself nothing dead or quite lifeless, this first offspring of his Being is necessarily a *two-fold substance,* inasmuch as it (speaking *anthropopathos,* or after the manner of men) consists of *the living word of the Father,* as the efficient or *working;* and then, secondly, of the passive substratum of the word which is as it were the Feminine of the Godhead, and serves him as the mirror wherein at once and from eternity he sees and recognizes the types and ideas of all merely possible creatures.

The *passivity* of wisdom is called in Scripture the "glory of God" (Exodus 16:10), inasmuch as from it, as from his inexhaustible treasury, he draws all his attributes of majesty, glory, wrath, vengeance, &c., which are impartable to the creatures. 1 Chron. 29:11. She is that fruitful mother who is above, by whom God is constantly accompanied, who is with him equally eternal, infinite, and omnipresent, and without whom he can impart himself to or be enjoyed in a conscious way, by no created being. From it, under the old covenant, God took the material of that incombustible fire in which he appeared to Moses. Exodus 3:2, Heb. 12:29. From it he formed that visible cloud which filled the Tabernacle, and from which he spoke mouth to mouth with our Egyptian brother-master. Yea, and without it the incarnation of the word would have been impossible, as we shall show in the proper place.

The outspoken wisdom is not only the dwelling of the word, but the passive part of the same contains also the potential matter of all that is made. The Father has made all by the Son. Eph. 3 : 9. Wisdom is a breath of the divine omnipotence—a reflection of the everlasting light—an unstained mirror of omnipotence, and an image of the divine goodness. In the Scripture she describes herself, Prov. 8, Rev. 19 : 13. In the womb of this wisdom the matter of creation is only potentially present. This potential matter becomes real matter, the essential foundation of the worlds of spirits and bodies, by means of the word through the agency of the " seven spirits" who constantly stand before the throne of God, and who are subordinated to him who has all power in heaven and in earth. Thus the leading strings, the middle of the whole creation, are in his hands. These seven spirits are called the " seven eyes of the Lamb, which are sent forth into all lands," Rev. 5 : 6. By means of these spirits, then, God, through his *glory* as the passive of the Godhead, brings forth all that is *not God*. In the co-operation of these spirits, the spirit of the word, and in this the primordial will of the Father, is the moving spring. That these spirits may co-operate with one another, their essential or primary powers must be different, else neither action nor reaction could take place. Therefore according to the number of these spirits, there are seven general primary powers, as well in temporal as in eternal nature, by means of which, outside of God all that is has received its being. Their manner of operation consists in this—that, according to the laws of their nature, in the potential matter of the object to be produced, they arouse reacting qualities—partly in order thus to bring forth a movable creature-life, according to the idea of the forming spirit, partly in order to render substantial the incorporeal life-matter ; for it is the unchangeable will of God that that which is invisible and spiritual in himself shall be presented corporeally, even as already his whole Godhead dwells bodily in Christ. It is difficult to express in our corporeal speech the individual operations of each of these seven spirits.

The first nature-spirit imparts to the matter of creation the *attractive* primary power, and the second, the *expansive* primary, which consequently are grounded in eternal nature, and constitute the innermost moving springs of the spiritual and corporeal worlds; yea, they present the principle or ground of all energizing creature-life, but with various modifications in the different orders of existence, as men, angels, vegetation, but without losing their central resemblance, also without losing the power of ascending the scale (or ladder) upon which they have descended, when this may become necessary according to the plan of the Creator. *The susceptibility of all corporeal things to become again spiritual* is an established and demonstrated principle in our secret school. Dissolution and corruption must take place before body can be exalted to spirit, for what we sow will not become alive unless it die, &c.

As there is a natural body, there is a spiritual. Adam was invested with natural life; the second Adam, on the other hand, has spiritual, &c. 1 Cor. 15. This spiritual life is the result of the seven spirits, or natural powers, of which we are here speaking. The attractive primary power is the origin of all matter and all corporeality, while the repulsive power is the origin of all dissolution, subtilization, and spirituality. When both work with equal power, they produce the *circular* motion, that wheel of nature (see James 3 : 6, Greek, τροχὸν), as the *third quality* of the matter of creation, which may be called the womb of creature life. In the midst of the operations of the fourth spirit, in the middle-point of the above mentioned wheel of nature, there arises a *flashing crucial intersection*, which fully generates creature life. This is quite developed in the following working periods of the fifth and sixth nature-spirit, and by the power of the seventh spirit is made steadfast, or fixed over its *substrato*. We must, as you see, dear brother, use some scholastic terms occasionally to express our meaning, our own tongue is so poor. Even with that assistance how little is effected in the way of explanation! [True!]

Most gladly would we make comprehensible to you the mysteries of the fourth natural quality, as by it is brought about the separation of light and darkness. We should, however, overstep the limits of a letter. So much we must say, that in the crucially intersecting flash of the fourth nature-form, the inaccessible light of the Godhead is communicated to the creature, or is again withdrawn from it. The three first natural powers are equally appropriate to angels and to men, for out of them are constituted the souls of angels as of men; but in the fourth form is the separating boundary between evil and good, light and darkness, life and death, amidst which is the freedom to choose one or the other. Life consisting of the three first forms, that of all free creatures, is called evil, in as far as it is viewed in its own nature, and is alienated from the life of God. The all-sufficient God is alone good, who in his Son imparts himself to creatures as a light, has life and immortality, and changes the darkness of the creature into light, life, and goodness. All this takes place at the cross, for, as already said, the life-centre in its innermost part presents a cross-like intersecting light-ray, from whose central point, so long as the creature stands in the divine order, the light of the Godhead streams forth and illuminates the ground of life, in itself dark. O the gentle, the beneficent cross! *The cross is the fountain of all true light;* and oh how gently, how full of blessing flowed this cross in the beginning from the hands of God! But Lucifer and Adam have changed it into a cross of torture, deprived of all truth and light, to which we are now fastened through our whole lives, and on which at last love itself must die, in order to make the faded light again radiant on the cross on which it was once quenched.

Behold, beloved cross-brother, so deep is the sign ground-ed which you bear, which you have received from us as your order-symbol. It reaches to the centre of all worlds, yea, it is conterminous with the very Godhead. Ah! surely must Jesus suffer all that he suffered; for at the cross was lost the life from God, and only at the cross could it be restored again. Luke 24: 26.

The operations of the seven spirits must not be considered as taking place *successively*, but *simultaneously*, in one and the same moment; nor are the objects mentioned to be conceived of as separate in place; they are spiritual, and so *penetrable*, able to work in and through one another without any displacement. With our corporeal and material bodies and modes of thought, it is impossible to give to another a correct idea of all this. It can be conceived in the spirit, but not expressed. Conceive of a substance animated with seven different powers, which incessantly produce one another *actu purissimo*, and are changed into one another; which so intimately interpenetrate one another as to form only a single highly simple whole, that is inseparable; thus you will get a feeble image of what we have endeavored to set forth. Add to this, that these seven powers are dominated by another power, which does not belong to their own essence, but guides and directs them according to its will, and illumines them with its independent light, and you will have an image of *a good creature;* take away this light-power, so that it remains in its own character, and you have *an evil creature.* To all this is applicable what the apostle says, 1 Cor. 2:15, "The spiritual man discerneth all things."

PART II.

The Chaos produced by the Fall of Lucifer, son of the Dawn, and his subject legions, was reduced to Kosmos by the Almighty, and prepared for the habitation of a new being to be created, viz., of Man.

He was designed to be a spectacle of wonder to the unfallen angelic choirs, a subject of bitterest envy to Satan, and a perennial fountain of indescribable blessedness to himself. The Almighty took his body from the quintessence of the new creation, his soul from eternal nature, and his spirit from the very spring of divine life, which He imparted to him by an animating breath, and thus constituted him a Triune being, which was consequently, in the strictest sense a living image of his own Godhead.

THE PERFECTIONS OF ADAM.—Shall we say, Adam was a God? That is indeed to say very much, and yet, nevertheless it is perfectly true. Not merely an angel, not at all a mere creature of the world of light—no, beloved, he was something more than this, he was a second Divinity, subordinate only to the Triune. The end of his being, his dignity, his nobility, his destination, were so perfect and exalted, that he surpassed all hitherto created spirits; for these two latter inhabit only the two inner spheres of creation, viz., the worlds of light and of fire; Adam, on the other hand, was *a confluence of the whole;* was an inhabitant of a threefold world, and consequently was present there also from where other blessed spirits are excluded, and, bowed in reverence, only long to gaze into. To understand this, recollect we have seen that in order to bring forth creatures God must awaken opposite qualities in eternal nature, that a creature-life different from his own may result. Now the sphere of these opposite or contrary vital powers, this fiery triangle in the midst of a quadrangle, constitutes a peculiar world for itself, which is called the dark world of fire, inasmuch as without the light inhabited by the spirit, it is thick darkness and gnawing, consuming fire. This world, which forms the ground of hell, and is present in the deepest interior of all creatures, had no inhabitant before the fall of Lucifer, but was merely the necessary basis of another world, which is called the domain of light—while in it the dark powers of fire were swallowed up of Light and anointed with the oil of the divine goodness. Now the world of light was the proper abode of all angels and spirits, and at the same time the throne of the divine spirit, which accordingly was built upon the ground of hell; for without the powers of the world of fire neither were creatures possible, nor could light itself have been raised to the splendor of the divine majesty, as, for illustration, we see that without the burning or consuming powers of fire earthly light can neither appear nor shine forth in its full brightness.

Besides these two worlds there was joined in Adam also the third, viz., this external visible world, as not only was his ethereal body formed out of the quintessence of the earth, but also even the divine breath by which God imparted to him life and motion, was a threefold existence partaking of all three worlds. This divine breath of life consisted namely, not only of the immortal fire-spirit and light-spirit of both the inner worlds, but also of the spirit of this outer world, yet all in the greatest harmony and order, so indeed that the fire-spirit and the world-spirit were subordinate to the spirit of the realm of light, by means of which also they had essential communion with the spirit of the word. How noble, how exalted, how divine was then the internal and external condition of this more than blessed creature! Like God, he was present in all three worlds; yet like God again, dwelt only in the angelic world of light. Besides, Adam was, only on a small scale, essentially three-in-one like God. Nay, more. He possessed indeed a three-fold tri-unity; for the above three worlds exist like their seven vital powers, one in another, and the most intimate centre of them all is God, in whom they are all destined to be swallowed up as in the consecrated decade or number *ten*.

The Godhead of Adam was shown on another side in the most splendid light. Like God, he was a being capable of bearing or producing from himself; for he possessed both the male and female powers of generation, powers which we will in future designate as the fire-tincture and the light-tincture. God created him a male and a female (Genesis 1 : 27), that is, he gave to Adam both faculties of propagation, and formed him a real masculine maiden. In this condition, it was intended that he should produce his kind in a magical way—that is, through the imaginative powers of attraction and chaste enkindling in the spirit of the word which he bore within him, the union of the fire-tincture and the light-tincture should take place for the generation of his race, in which no animal organs or vessels would be needed, seeing that the embryo produced by this heavenly union would come to light immediately and in its entire perfection, without having passed through the many stages of development necessary to the completion of every animal offspring. In brief, not from blood or from the will of the flesh, but in, through, and from God, Adam would have begotten an innumerable posterity. He was in general like the angels and blessed spirits, who neither marry nor are given in marriage for the propagation of their kind, but in the chaste embrace of *Sophien* (wisdom), the general mother who is above, are prolific, and propagate themselves in a magical supersensual way.

And what shall we say of the external Godhead of Adam? As all that is created is subjected to the omnipotence of the Infinite, and is dependent on his orders, so to Adam were subject all spheres of the external world, and he without restraint ruled over all that God had separated and brought forth from the deteriorated elements of chaos ; for in order to impart to him this dominion in the fullest measure, God created him out of the purest quintessence of the whole outer creation, for the reason that without this inestimable advantage such dominion could not have continued, nay, would not have been possible. Thus the influences of the inner realm of Light came to his support, and as he possessed the magic power of vision, so also he possessed an infallible knowledge of the properties and distinctive marks of all things, by aid of which he bestowed upon them their appropriate names. (Gen. 2 : 20.) The animal nature was already manifest in innumerable animals ; but his (Adam's) own animality was present in him only potentially, and most deeply concealed in the temperature of light; whence it follows, that to him only the way of the imagination was left in which he could sin—that is, depart from his dependence on God and become unfaithful to his Spirit, seeing that his powers of generation were not yet separated, and he consequently had as yet no external helper with whom he could —as some would affirm—unite himself in a corporeal manner and after the way of animals. To wish for this, or imagine himself in this, was all he could do—and which, alas! compelled God, through the separation of the power of light, to give him the longed-for helper.

In reference to the other functions (or parts) of animality, he needed as little any animal organs, either for the digestion of food eaten, or for the separation of heterogeneous portions, He enjoyed, indeed, of all; but ever only paradisaical fruit and with paradisaical mouth, in which likewise was the central point of the faculties of separation, by means of which the things enjoyed were indeed tasted, but also dissolved with the gentlest sensation, and each conveyed back into its own domain. Of what use would have been the animal stomach and intestines, with the other instruments of assimilation, when not only no revealed curse was present, but the Adamic appetite for nourishment was directed solely upon paradisaical power-essence—that is, upon things which existed in the most perfect temperature of light, and were consequently indestructible? As to the perfection of his external and internal senses, this is beyond all present conception of man lying under the curse—for while the subjects, the objects of these senses, were partly divine, partly paradisaical, necessarily the senses to be affected by them must possess a corresponding power of apprehension and receptivity. But who are men, dearest brother, that they should be able to give account of a matter which to them is more utterly lost than to the unhappy father of our race himself? How should blind moles speak fitly of the splen· dor of the sun, and beings born in darkness declare the majesty of the beneficent radiance of light?

It was a part of the Adamic Godhead that the elements of the external world were wholly under his command. His body had not the clumsy gravity of ours, nor was it bound down to the sluggish clods that press so many drops of sweat from our brows; therefore he moved through the air and through the water without difficulty; not only so, he visited the deepest bowels of the earth to refresh his spirit in the view of their manifold treasures. The mobility of his body was like the swiftness of his thoughts, and his will was inviolable law for the elements, as also for the creatures formed from them; they were incapable of making injurious impressions upon him, inasmuch as he was created in an invulnerable condition, was endowed with penetrability (the susceptibility of being passed through by another body), and could neither be touched nor hurt by anything outside of himself. Physical evil, with its numberless consequences, was to him utterly unknown, and to guard against moral evil was also in his power. He was subject to no corporeal necessities; he stood in want of nothing; he was naked without knowing it, as he was invested with light which shone from within him and filled his whole atmosphere with light and love—like the glorification of Jesus on Mount Tabor. The internal and external energies of his soul knew no weariness or exhaustion such as the powers of our present bodies experience, which we are compelled to resuscitate in sleep—a state resembling death. The heavenly bodies, indeed, by their revolution, formed day and night; but both were alike to Adam, who was raised above all changes of external nature; for he was sun and moon to himself, he had essentially in himself that light which shines from without upon those creatures who live under the dominion of the world-spirit; yea, he bore within himself the purest extract, or quintessence of all outer constellations. Light was his outer garment, and from within again streamed other modifications of the principle of light through the pores of his ethereal body, visible to the naked eye—as not only the pores but the whole bodily structure of Adam were endowed with the most perfect diaphaneity.

But when should we finish enumerating all the great unspeakable advantages which the highest Master-Builder had conjoined in the body of Adam? We have already said much, but how little in comparison with what is not said.

For we have said nothing of the aptitudes of his spirit, of his magical way of knowledge, his exalted understanding, his unlimited insight into the being of things ; nothing of his intimate intercourse with God, and the inner world of spirits, of his capability of growth in the divine life, and generally nothing of his adaptation for that nameless blessedness, happiness, and fullness of God, which awaited him when through the good use of his freedom he should have rendered to God the homage required of him. But what mortal dare presume himself qualified for the treatment of these subjects, without being himself a God, or at least Adam?

In order finally to render the Godhead of Adam complete, God imparted to him also unlimited freedom of will, such as he had once given to the reigning Princes, now fallen. This prerogative which assimilated him to the most exalted spirits of the inner world, was designed to qualify him to receive from the hand of his Maker the manifold treasures of blessedness that he enjoyed and should continue to enjoy, not merely as a mechanical gift, but as a reward of his reciprocal love and faithfulness. With respect to this, trial was necessary in order to see whether or not Adam would persevere, out of free love to God, in the heavenly sphere in which he was created, and so render himself worthy of his blessedness. The Divine Light had united these in itself to a jubilant reciprocation of affection. The dark world of fire delighted in the holy world of light, and these again in the external world as their revelation *ad extra*. Thus was Adam the theatre of a three-fold fundamental impulse or inclination, which, however, by means of the light possessed the most perfect unity. But outside of him this unity of light did not exist in so high a degree, for both the world of fire and the outer creation were already broken off from the realm of light, and had established themselves in their own possession, although the outer world was still in some measure dominated by the inner realm of light, and held in bounds. Even by this state of things was the Adamic freedom to be put to the test, viz., into which of these three worlds it in imagination would enter. The garden in Eden was appointed for this trial—a place of our planet where God allowed the holy element of the inner world *to bloom forth* through the earth to produce paradisaical fruits for Adam.

ADAM'S TRIAL AND FALL.—The trial itself was three-fold; for each one of the three worlds obtained permission, as it were, to attempt to gain a victory over the other two in Adam. To these were joined the envy and malice of the fallen Angel, who put forth all his strokes of art to involve Adam in his own fate, and to secure the issue for the kingdom of darkness. However, on the side of the dark world of fire, which alone permitted free access to him as its inhabitant, he could effect nothing. Adam was too well entrenched, and was surrounded with a two-fold breast-work, viz., of outer and inner light, by which he frustrated all attempts to raise against him the powers of fire. Satan therefore abandoned his first purpose, and now endeavored to render Adam at least susceptible to the enticements of the external world, and thus ruin his happiness in another way. He therefore inflamed his imagination—showed him, as to our Lord in the wilderness, all the kingdoms, beauties, and witcheries of the world; described the pleasure of knowing good and evil; caused him to long for one like himself in order to propagate himself like those animals who live under the spirit of the world; in brief, he called to his aid all that the Scripture comprehends under "the lust of the eye, the lust of the flesh, and the pride of life," in order to gain the victory over him. And, alas! his devilish toil was not in vain; for he had struck the weak side of Adam, who, caught in this net, lost his harmony with the kingdom of light, and along with this his whole godhood. For as soon as he imagined himself in the enjoyment of this lure, his desires, his volition, his magical power of representation, were fettered and become the slave of the object to which he had turned his affection, as the direction of his will. This was Adam's first transgression, from which the loss of the magical power of propagation was the necessary consequence. For as soon as he so grossly misused his freedom as to let himself be dragged by his imagination into animal nature, generation out of God—who is so jealous of his honor—could not possibly take place. Whenever God saw that, through Adam's sin, matters were come to such a pass that his honor and holiness did not permit him to remain so closely united with him, He—who in the beginning had pronounced all which he had made, "very good"—said, "It is not good that man should continue longer alone, else he may lose himself yet more, and render himself still more unworthy of my grace." He therefore let him feel the first consequence of his sin while he threw him into a deep sleep — which in his state of innocence had not been possible—and deprived him of his feminine power of propagation. He also lost the heavenly indwelling of *Sophien* at the time God created for him a helper with whom he could gratify his false desire and propagate himself in an animal way. As soon as he saw her he recognized her for flesh of his flesh—an irresistible proof that God had made him a male and a female, that is, had united in him the male and female generative powers.

ADAM AFTER THE FALL.—With what abyss of distraction and misery shall we let our pen, dipped in tears, begin to be the recorder of Adam's history? Shall we take the material of our lamentations from within, or from without? Was body, soul, or spirit more injured, rendered more void of their Godhood, and more thrust down, more deeply degraded, from the throne of their original nobility? Alas! the whole Adam, the whole Eve, were equally wounded, saw themselves surrounded by the goads and stings of one and the same Death and Hell, and had now the additional mortification of being mocked by God and by the Devil. "See then," it was said, "Adam is become as one of us." Gen. 3:22. The deadly mouthful indeed did not operate at once. After its enjoyment Eve still had time to persuade her husband also to a like transgression. But it operated the more certainly, the more its operation allowed them time to satisfy their whole desire upon it. Now, however, unhappy Adam! blinded Eve! this costly mouthful is swallowed; already its poison is creeping through the innermost passages of your ethereal body; it is mingling with the most subtile juices full of paradisaic light; it is imparting to them the leaven which will cause their dissolution, the separation of their qualities; with mortal* tooth it is gnawing at the pillar of the divine life, and without immediate consciousness, the animal nature is beginning to unfold itself, to turn itself outward, and from possibility to attain o reality, and to subordinate the Life of Light to the domain of the external world-spirit.

Pitiable progenitors of a whole humanity still buried in the chaos of the future! What will shortly become of you? Your divine light from within is losing its radiant splendor. The animating glance of the Water of Light is visibly swallowed up by the predominating Ground of Fire. The image of God grows dim. The Spirit of the Word, which hitherto possessed you as the king of all humanity, withdraws back into the divine abyss. The magical power of vision is changed into animal shortsightedness and deceptive night. Your spiritual power of propagation passes over into animal generative appetite, full of shame and sorrow, and all your spiritual aptitudes are converted into obtuse sensuous feeling. Unhappy Adam, whither art thou falling? Outwardly, after the loss of thy clothing of light, thou feelest the nakedness of a hateful animal body, of which thou hast the more to be ashamed the greater it is in comparison with all other animals. The four external elements, since thou hast lost and broken up their temperature, storm against thee without restraint; heat, cold, and all the disagreeablenesses of entire external nature, make thee the target of their rage; and hunger and thirst, and all the corporeal needs of the most rugged animal, are now thy lot. In order to digest animal food,

* " Whose *mortal* taste, &c." See Milton.—*Trans.*

and to separate the everywhere diffused curse from the pure portion of the means of nourishment, thou possessest now a stomach and entrails ; and in order to propagate a race like thyself, to thee, and to thee alone among all animal creatures, are given organs which are associated with shame. Instead of being able to move thy body freely through all elements without hindrance, thou art so utterly bound to the earthly burden of thy animal body, that almost every step causes thee to shed a drop of sweat, forces from thee a sigh. Formerly thy ethereal body was the pure quintessence of all animality ; now it is degraded to an animal of all animals; yea, instead of reigning over all animals, thou art now their general slave. In future, thou wilst daily through animal sleep renew the image of thy death in the inner spiritual life, and the outward sun, which fortunately for thee is still there, will never go down to thee, without, to thy ever-enduring sorrow, reminding thee of the eternal day which formerly shone upon thee. Poor Adam, worthy of compassion, where art thou ? Whither hast thou wandered ? Already the measure of thy unhappiness is so full; how will it be when first the judgments of God upon thee shall awake ? When also God himself shall exercise righteousness upon thee? What says to thee, even now, thy inexorable conscience ?

The divine threat—on the day thou eatest thereof death shall be the consequence—was only too punctually fulfilled. They truly died—not, indeed, that death which now robs men of their animal life. Alas ! that odious animal was as yet by no means developed in them. They died in the inner life, as to essential communion with God, and on the other hand, fell within the realm of the outer world, which Jesus names the kingdom of darkness, and which the apostle names the region of the air, ruled by Lucifer. Dying is nothing else but *the separation of the principles of life*, of which death is the necessary consequence. Now Adam was made in the kingdom of light. His ethereal body was the habitation of the two inner worlds ; and as the purest extract of the earth which was found in the solar point of terrestrial natural light, the elements of this body existed in the most absolute harmony—which invested him, as to his body, with the immortality which he already possessed as to his soul. But the unfortunate indulgence of their appetite for delicate food had ruined them (Adam and Eve) with respect to both, had separated both bonds. They first died as to the inner life from God, and after they had borne long enough the consequences of their sin, bodily death also followed, as the inheritance of all the children of Eve who should be begotten after the flesh. In the strictest understanding, they also died a three-fold death: first, in (or, as to) the inner kingdom of light, which retired back again into its holy darkness, and left them in their own— namely, in the lightless abyss of fire. Then ensued the dissolution of their ethereal body into its contradictory elements—by means of which they not only became suscep- tible of the influence of the spirit of the outer world and of the four elements, but also, as already said, had the misfor- tune to see themselves changed into an animal of all animals—in the full meaning of the word—as their animal- ity was the aggregate of all animal attributes. Finally, this animal must also die, and go the way of all flesh, as it is impossible that flesh and blood should either see, or ever again possess, the kingdom of God, which Adam lost through his separation from the world of light. 1 Cor. 15: 20.

This, dearest brother, was the mournful end of the Adamic Fall. As an animal, he was now no more suscep- tible of the paradisaic life of light, and therefore according to his condemnation he was banished not only from Eden, but also from all Paradise—that is to say, out of the tem- perature of the Holy Element.

We must know Paradise was a certain place of our planet, where God allowed the holy element to bloom greenly through the four external elements, as the abode of animals —in which also paradisaic fruits were produced—and changed this locality into a heavenly garden full of splendor and manifold beauty. It was the purpose of God, that in proportion as man multiplied his race in a magical way, Paradise should gradually be extended from this place, until it should by degrees cover the whole earth. But unhappily by the abuse of his freedom man reduced himself to an animal, and thus frustrated the views of his Maker, as he became incapable of multiplying in Paradise, or of longer enjoying it. For even after his separation into man and woman, he might still have propagated in Paradise, if by eating the forbidden fruit he had not utterly deprived himself of the privilege. Hence it is clear that Adam committed a two-fold sin. His first offense was the imagination of animal propagation, of which the separation of the feminine power of light, or the formation of Eve, was the consequence; and the enjoyment of the forbidden fruit was a second sin independent of the former—upon which followed the development of the animal nature, the evolution of the curse, and the utter loss of Paradise; notwithstanding that Adam had as yet by no means known his helper carnally, else his first-born Cain could not possibly have carried with him a fratricidal impulse; an irresistible proof that he was not begotten by Adam in Paradise.

We have shown that is was simply *the inseparable possession of God* which Adam lost in the fall. It was God himself, the Spirit of his Word who essentially possessed him in light; who ruled him, embraced him in love as his bride, furnished him all his goods and treasures; briefly! it was God himself, his light, his love, his essential communion, wherein the life and the nobility of Adam consisted. Consequently there neither has been nor is outside of this God any created being, not even the highest seraph, capable of retrieving or compensating Adam's loss; for even the most exalted of all blessed spirits is only from and out of God that which he is; and therefore if he were so unhappy as, like Adam, to forsake the divine communion, he could obtain his restoration only from God himself; as it is impossible that any finite being can serve as a vehicle of the Infinite.

Weigh well, brother, what we say, and impress it deeply on your memory, for we have uttered a truth so ponderous that it alone is sufficient to countervail all your doubts in regard to the divinity of Jesus. We therefore repeat it: *what Adam possessed was God, and what he lost in the fall was also God, with whom through wisdom he was essentially united.* God is that illimitable sea of blessedness wherein all angels and spirits are more or less immerged, and in which alone they are and abide, blessed, holy, good, righteous—or in one word, in which they are and continue even Gods so long as they do not issue from it in imagination. Suppose, now, that one of these divinities were so unhappy as to abandon the fountain of life—or, abiding by our similitude, to go out of the divine sea of infinity—tell us, brother, whether any other being that swims in this sea, would be able to restore Godhood to the apostate creature? Or still more plainly say, whether it were, if we may thus speak, in the power of God's omnipotence, to employ creatures so limited that they are hardly competent to grasp so much of the divine essence as is required for their own salvation, as a means by which to imbue again an entire humanity with light and with the fulness of God? *No, brother; that which neither has nor can receive, cannot impart to others.* The Seraph is perhaps the being most full of divinity, the humanity of Jesus excepted ; but he nevertheless possesses only a creatural measure of it, and is only as a mote in a sunbeam to the sun. Assuming also that it involved no impossibility, that a creature could receive as much as were required, and could also impart it to others— yet *could it never receive the whole Godhead*, which the Father of all had resolved to introduce into fallen humanity. This reaches away beyond all power of the creature, and is only the property of Wisdom in the Word—which is co-eternal with God, equally infinite, so long as it has not passed over into nature and creation.

This is, indeed mere stammering, dear brother; however, see to it well, what we have here said, as it were in passing, and in our stammering speech you will find truth full of unction. When doubts in regard to the deity of Jesus assail you, forget not that only wisdom dwelling outside of nature and creation, equally eternal and infinite with God, is or can be receptive of the whole Godhead. This truth we declare incontestible, and boldly challenge all reason to overthrow it. That, however, the purpose of God was to impart his whole divine fulness to separated humanity, is clear —partly from his nature, which is indivisible, consequently in every instance can and must be imparted entire though gradually—and partly from the need of man, whom God in the very beginning so constructed that out of God absolutely he can be satisfied with nothing else.

But let us return to the history of Adam. It would surely have been impossible for him to recover his lost inheritance, if God had not come to his aid. And oh! the incomprehensible goodness! Already before Adam's creation this loving Father had provided for the possible abuse of human freedom, in a manner which must draw tears of love and joy from the least feeling creature. For even before the foundation of the earth was laid we were chosen in Christ, the bruiser of the serpent; that is to say, even before God had restored to order the chaos produced by the fall of Lucifer. He resolved, in case man should fail in his trial, nevertheless to carry out his decree, and to introduce again into humanity the whole treasure of his love and compassion in and through the only saving name of Jesus. Eph. 1: 4. Moreover, God, according to the Fire-abyss of the dark world, had known beforehand that Adam would fall, and had therefore determined beforehand the means of restoration. Oh the boundless goodness and love of our God! Who will give us the mouth of all created worlds, that we may be able sufficiently to adore, magnify and laud him? Truly, brother, if God had already possessed no such exalted means of recovery in the treasure of his wisdom, he would never have exposed man, by his creation, to the peril of rendering himself irretrievably miserable.

God showed Adam still another favor which may stand by the side of the former, namely: as he foresaw that Adam would have to undergo the sharpest temptation from the envy of Lucifer, he left in him from the distracted chaos, a little tinder, a small unregenerate particle, which should serve him as a counterpoise, when during the trial Satan might draw him somewhat more toward the inner world of fire than toward outward animal life: for, however wretched the fate of humanity became through the latter, yet it would have been much more miserable, if Adam had, like Lucifer, grasped after the inner world of fire. Take notice, beloved brother, even when the purpose not in any degree to encroach upon human freedom, necessitates the Creator to permit evil to take place, yet he seeks beforehand in the most amiable way to mitigate it. How unutterably miserable our condition would have been, if we, with Lucifer, had fallen into the power of the abyss of fire! We are miserable, but we have a Saviour who, through the partaking of his flesh and blood, will impart to us again the lost spiritual life, the temperature of light. John 6: 53. Besides, we also now live in a very tolerable habitation. We have the earthly sun which illumines us, and the external light of nature which for brief moments can satisfy the hunger of our souls. The variety and beauty of the productions of the earth, the animal and vegetable kingdoms, the changing seasons of the year, and even all the four elements, have for us something beneficent: and the general spirit of the world, how busy is this in entertaining our senses with innumerable juggleries! What an inestimable advantage we enjoy in the single circumstance, that through this earthly life, God offers us a means, at once short and frequently sweetened with his grace, of attaining to regeneration by the hand of Jesus! All this, and infinitely more than this, we know or understand, must Satan dispense with in his dark prison-house; and we also, after our earthly life, shall have a like fate, unless we take with us into eternity the life of Jesus, unless we shall be born anew from above out of water and spirit.

How kindly also did God provide for Adam, notwithstanding the antecedent knowledge of his unfaithfulness!

It is also to be seen in the whole history of Adam, how obviously this counterpoise always operated with him; for Lucifer soon saw that on the side of the Fire-abyss nothing could be effected, and therefore he directed his dark powers outward, where both worlds were still good and evil in disjunction.

Part III.

The Restoration of our Fallen Humanity in Christ.

The divine conduct toward Adam after the fall is known from the books of Moses. We learn that when he had withdrawn himself a whole birth from God and his light, and now, in deep grief for his nakedness, wove aprons, God summoned him to account, cursed the serpent as the unhappy instrument of the seduction; and after he had delivered the sentence of his sufferings and death, he made him the consolatory promise, that he would place enmity between the seed of the woman and that of the serpent, and through the former, would finally subjugate and destroy the whole kingdom of death and darkness. Gen. 3 : 15. This was an unexpected lesson for the mocking spirit of lies; for though, as an inhabitant of the dark world, he had, like God, foreseen the consequences of Adam's fall, and even learned them by his own experience, yet according to the divine abyss of light, as to which he had died before Adam's creation, it was impossible for him even to guess, much less to anticipate, the divine means of restoration. Even the loving mouth which before uttered curse and mortality, now gave expression to life and blessedness. *The speech of God is, however, the most perfect doing.* In the moment also in which God uttered the aforesaid promise, he again essentially imparted himself *in and through Jehovah* to the extinguished Light-abyss in Eve, as an immortal pledge of his promise; imperceptible, however, to the animal senses and understanding, as in a quite foreign land, and unable to attain again to their inheritance without mystical as well as corporeal death. This impartation did not accrue to the Fire-abyss of Adam, but to the extinguished Light-abyss in the womb of Eve, as it alone had receptivity for *the spirit of the vivifying word,* and so could properly be the dwelling place of the same. Besides God had resolved *through a real humanifying of his only begotten Son,* to reconsecrate the feminine light-essence, and thereby restore again the divine image in all mankind. Therefore the love of the Father again came forth from the divine Triad, and anew married itself with the extinguished light-tincture of Eve. This adorable memorial of the divine compassion was like glimmering tinder, an undying spark of light, which was capable of kindling into love all the seven powers of life of the abyss of fire, and in general of re-establishing in all humanity the lost kingdom of light. Even this celestial life-spark is that grain of mustard seed, that leaven, to which Jesus likened the kingdom of God—or, to say all in a word, *it is the living seed of the divine kingdom* which all men without distinction receive; which, however, with most of them, falls among thorns, or into otherwise unfruitful ground. Matt. 13 : 33, Luke 8 : 11, 1 Peter 1 : 23, Matt. 13 : 24. This divine seed of life was transplanted through Eve into her sons and daughters, and through them, from generation to generation, even to the blessed point of time when the Life and Light himself appeared (*vita erat lux.* John 1), in order to enlighten and vivify all men whom the will of the flesh had begotten in and for the outward animal world. But as light can subjugate darkness, and life can subjugate death in no other way than by overcoming them in contest—both, however, sometimes conquer, sometimes are conquered—so did it happen in this case. The light indeed possessed sufficient superiority of strength and power to overcome all opposition, and to be victorious everywhere—of which we have a speaking illustration in the sudden conversion of Saul, Acts 9 : 4; but man's free will, which God permitted still to continue after the fall, embarrassed the light in the employment of its omnipotence; for God will have no people under constraint, he will have them enjoy the utmost freedom of will. Lev. 23 : 88, 2 Chron. 17 : 16. Hence it has happened, that, ever since men have existed, the divine light-spark has, without cessation, sometimes prevailed, sometimes been overcome. As it has also not seldom happened that the light gained the upper hand already in the transplantation and production of the soul, it becomes quite comprehensible how God could hate the Esaus on the one side, and love the Jacobs on the other, even before their birth. O brother, what a happiness then it is to be born of pious parents! How numerous are the examples of unhappy souls, who owe their existence merely to the tumultuous desire of the flesh! Alas! of those begotten under the cross the instances are too few, else we should certainly be in a position to draw the most convincing parallels.

Through the two ways in which the divine spark of life was transplanted arose among the posterity of Adam *two lines of birth*, viz., the line of light, and then the line of the world-spirit, or of darkness. Both uninterruptedly run parallel with each other. The former brought forth the children of God, the latter brought forth the daughters and the sons of men. Rom. 9 : 8, Rom. 8 : 14, &c. Eve was indeed the original possessor of the light glimmering up again in darkness ; but the world-spirit nevertheless proved his first claim on her children; for Cain, the first-born of Eve, of whom she even believed that in him she possessed already the man Jehovah who should bruise the serpent's head, was a fratricide. Abel, her second son, first gave its beginning to the line of life, which was propagated continuously beside the former, to Mary, the purest of virgins. At last appeared the long wished for world-day of four thousand years, which, in the counsels of God (as the fourth day of creation was destined for the concentration of the outward natural light in the orb of the sun), was appointed for the revelation in human nature of the Word as the sun of the world of spirits. All heaven, the whole world of light, prepared for the novel spectacle, in which the compassionate love of the Father assumed so incomprehensible and so humiliating a character. The most important embassage possible between heaven and earth, between God and his creature, was constituted. Gabriel, in the name of the Most High, must solicit the free human will of Mary for her consent to the incarnation of the Word in her person. After a short consultation with herself, she consents ; submits entirely to the good pleasure of God; is hereupon filled with the Spirit of the Word ; the power of the Most High, that is, his glory as the embodied power, or the passivity of the Godhead, overshadows her maidenly light-ground, wherein the Spirit of the Word, through excitation of the magical igneous triangle, of which we have spoken above, forms a real masculine soul of fire, imbues the same likewise with its divine light, constructs for both out of the holy element, an ethereal body, connects the same also with a body out of the four elements, and finally it is born as a real man. This, dearest brother, is that unspeakable mystery of the love of our God, whose breadth, depth, and weight are greater than the creaturely understanding will be able to comprehend even in eternity ; yea, greater than the making of a thousand systems of worlds; for these are the result of firmly established laws, which are comprehensible, at least by higher intelligences, and even depend upon their guidance. But the incarnation of Him whom the seraphim trembling adore, without being able to comprehend even the very least of his depths, this is an abysm of all abysms, a bottomless gulf into which even the most exalted world of angels cannot look without being lost. And, beloved brother, can we, filled with holy horror, under the strongest feeling of awe and thankfulness, do less than keep silence? Eph. 3 : 18, John 14, 1 Cor. 4 : 9.

The Word, or the first-born before every creature, and God of God, revealed himself in the flesh thereby that he himself became flesh, and combined miserable, pitiable, bewildered humanity with his eternal Godhead, in the view to replace the awakened wrath of the world of fire in the kingdom of light, to reunite the separated principles of life, and to reconcile the enraged justice of the Father through regeneration. Under this fleshly veil the God-man grew up like other sons of Adam; he waxed in favor with God and men; he was subject to his parents; for thirty years he led a poor, obscure, self-denying life; he finally stepped forth as the Son and ambassador of his heavenly Father ; he taught his brethren the vital truths up to that time for the most part concealed; he showed them that the salvation of his sheep made it necessary that he should shed his blood and give his life for them ; he also confirmed his words by the fearless offering of himself, as after a course of the most cruel maltreatment, between two murderers* who were preferred to him, he died on the infamous cross, praying for those who crucified him. Luke 2 : 52, 2 Sam. 7 : 14, Rom. 8 : 3, Matt. 17 : 12, Mark 15 : 27, Luke 23 : 34. This was the tragical end of the God-man, at whose birth heaven kept novel festival, and whom during his life the inhabitants of the angelic world strove in rivalry to wait upon, with the reverence due to God.

Yea, the Word became flesh, and we have seen his glory under a human veil. The Word, which in the beginning was with God, yea, which was, is, and shall be God himself, by a hypostatical inseparable union of the Godhead with human nature, hath kindled again the spark of life transplanted from Eve to Mary ; hath anointed the wrath of nature with the oil of gentleness ; hath changed hell into heaven, darkness into light, death into life and immortality, and in general, hath again re-established the image of God, the inner kingdom of light, first in his own person, and then also in the souls of those firstlings of the faith, who in the moment of his death flowed together into one with him in the newly opened abyss of life, being the first members of the body of Jesus, and appeared to many citizens of Jerusalem. The necessity of the sufferings of Jesus was also grounded in eternal nature; for know you not, said Jesus

---

* Luther's version, Mark 15 : 27.—*Trans.*

himself, that Christ must suffer all that in order to enter into his glory? Luke 24 : 26. Say not the prophets the same? Has not the Spirit in manifold ways declared it beforehand? and have ye not learned from the Mosaic offerings, that the Anointed of God could enter into the Holy of Holies only through the shedding of his blood, only through the sacrifice of himself?

Alas! O Jesus! thou well namest us fools and beings of slow and hard hearts. How blind, how insensible we are, without the influence of thy grace, in regard to everything pertaining to God. We have broken ourselves off by a whole birth from thee and from thy kingdom of light. Our spirit, soul, and body are equally corrupt, equally empty of all that can satisfy our magical fire-hunger. Nevertheless we feel not our loss, and are seized with sadness when we see that in order to place the Light again on the throne, the birth of the flesh, even in thee, O divine brother-master, must necessarily die, and all the seven powers of life (which out of connection with thee are only miserable slaves of the world-spirit) must be brought to dissolution and corruption. For be assured, most beloved brother, that the proposition, *the dissolution of the one is the foundation for the bearing of the other*, is general, and especially applies to the regeneration of man, and indeed the more certainly in proportion as the same has operated on the person of Christ. Besides, how could or should the disciple be more favored than the master? Matt. 10 : 24. Nay, brother, even there must you pass through where your Master has gone before, let flesh and blood revolt at it as they may. Remember that you are a brother of the cross, that you have sworn to the consecrated gibbet, which is folly to the heathen, an offense to the Jew, and a stone of stumbling to the nominal Christian.

Comprehend it well, dear brother, wherein the work of redemption through Christ peculiarly consisted. First, by a natural birth through Mary, God combined the lost principle of light with human nature in Christ. The Godhead of

Jesus was consequently united with a real or true human soul, and this with a human spirit and body. He took upon himself all the seven degenerate powers of life, without, however, becoming participant in their sinful outgoings; was in all points tempted like as we are; however, he steadfastly overcame the temptation to sin, as yonder in the wilderness, through the inner power of his Godhead, and finally allowed the tinder of sin utterly to perish by the most painful death of the body. These lifeless ashes, this dead matter he revivified anew with his divine spirit of light, he thus transmuted (*tingirte**) the dead curse into life and light; he restored the principles of the outer body to their former temperature; he thus reopened lost Paradise, and glorified his external body into that luminous, resplendent, celestial body which formerly he had permitted partially to show radiant on Mount Tabor; with it he passed through closed doors, walked on the water, ruled the elements, and finally returned into the bosom of his Father, in order to send the spirit of truth to his germinating community-body (his church). John 20: 26, Mark 6: 48, Matt. 8: 27, *et al.*, John 16: 13. How true it is, therefore, that as through the sin of one condemnation came upon all men, &c. Rom. 5: 18, 1 Cor. 15: 22. For as we all die in Adam, so shall we all be made alive in Christ.

Dear brother, these are surely comforting, beneficent, bliss-breathing truths. However, all this took place in that time only in the humanity of Christ, and all the other children of Adam who, through faith in the promised Messiah, had not been engrafted into the tree of life, remained, even as such remain to-day, buried in sin and under the curse. For Christ in the human nature has not mitigated the paternal wrath in such a sense, that it is enough for us to know in a historical way what he did, and to believe, or at most to confess ourselves sinners, that we may expect confidently an interest in his merits, and at the same time retain the old man

---

Tingiren, in the phraseology of the Alchemists, ment to transmute, as one metal into another.—*Trans.*

with his animal appetites, and daily nourish them to greater power. Oh no, beloved! That is the most dangerous and yet, alas! the most common of all self-deception; for it is simply an irrefragable, though for the life of the animal man, a terrible truth—whosoever loves his own life or his soul will lose it, but whosoever for Jesus' sake shall lose it, shall save it unto life eternal. Matt. 10: 30, Mark 8: 35, Luke 17: 33, John 12 : 25. This is of course a fearful lesson for the life of the flesh, a lesson which forced the sweat of overwhelming anguish even from the God-man. However, not a syllable of its contents shall fail. *Every thing which took place in Christ externally and internally must take place on a smaller scale in us also, though in a spiritual way.* In us also must Christ become a man—must bring forth his Godhead essentially in us; all the seven powers of life through the sword of the cherub which guards the entrance into Paradise, he must slay, must then revivify them with the breath of his Spirit, must raise them from the dead, and exalt them with him to heaven. Then first, dear brethren, the merits of Christ are in essence reckoned to our account, as we then essentially feel within us the fruits of the same, viz., the satisfaction of our dark soul-hunger as that wherein even the true forgiveness of sins consists. Also, then first are we real Christians, or better, little Jesuses and living members of his body, as we are inseparably united with him, as the branches are united with the vine; only from him draw sap and nourishment, and as true sheep, hear, love, and follow his voice.

You see, children, wherefore Jesus said, if ye eat not the flesh of the Son of man, and drink not his blood, ye have no life in you; for in this glorified flesh and blood dwells the whole fullness of the Godhead bodily. It is that general tincture of life, that panacea which Jesus, the loving chemist, prepared in and out of himself amidst the bitterest suffering on the cross. With this divine tincture we must be interpenetrated, we must mingle it essentially with ourselves; we must really enjoy this precious flesh and blood;

not, however, merely with the animal mouth, also not with respect to the gross external animal of burden, as which it is irrevocably destined to a death of corruption. *Our soul has its own mouth*, which stands in no connection with the animal mouth, and which can open when the latter is shut. This mouth is *the magical desire, the soul's power of attraction, the hunger and thirst for heavenly bread and the water of life*, which alone can permanently satisfy this magical vortex of fire. Even this magical desire, when united with confidence and love, is called living faith, to which all things are possible, and without which Jesus himself could have wrought no miracles ; for it is a particle of the divine power out of eternal nature, wanting which even God would not be omnipotent. Its peculiarity is that whatever it grasps in imagination, it holds fast, attracts, appropriates, and unites with its own nature, and also modifies it according to its own prevailing quality. To love is also the same as to enjoy. Into whatever, accordingly, the soul loves, eats thereof, and nourishes itself therewith—into whatever the soul enjoys—it will be transformed. Adam imagined himself into the animal principle, and became an animal. Earthly animal men imagine according to vanity, according to whatever flatters their sensuality and originates from the spirit of this world ; heavenly men, on the contrary, trample nature under foot, imagine, to the exclusion of everything else, in the spirit of Jesus, their divine lover, whom they attract through the magnetism of their souls, grasp in faith, and allow themselves to be essentially possessed by him. Through whatever may encounter them in this world they look to him alone. *Jesus is the spirit of their spirit, and the life of their life.* Out of him there is neither will, nor power, nor knowledge, nor desire, for them. They are dead to the world and to whatever is not Jesus, their life is hid with Christ in God. For they only, beloved brother, are true children of God who are born of God and are impelled by the Spirit of God. One, therefore, who has not the Spirit of Christ, is none of his, is no Christian; and may not expect, either in this world or the next, the inheritance of true Christians.

Oh that we could sufficiently impress upon your hearts the peculiar and essential thing in genuine Christianity as the only infallible way to the treasures of both lights. No hypocrisy, no merely external imputation of the merits of Christ is of any avail—as is very generally taught and believed. Either to die with Christ and rise again with him, or to be cast out into uttermost darkness, one of these two things is our inevitable doom. There is no third, no middle way between the two. Either all or nothing, life or death, light or darkness, are the two extremes which are submitted to our choice; and although, of course, in the eternal fields there are stages of purification, by means of which there may still be roads from one utmost limit to the other, yet they will merely serve to fix us in one of the two extremes for long eternities. Whatever of the merit of Jesus we do not really feel within us, do not experience in our own soul, does not touch us, and is an affair which takes place outside of us and is alien to our heart. The spirit of Jesus himself must really utter within us the comforting words : Son, be of good courage, thy sins are forgiven thee. Matt. 9 : 2. Then first, brother, then first we begin to be Christians, and come the more joyfully to Jesus, that we may be quickened by him. Mere knowledge without practice is of no avail.

Christ alone then makes us true Christians, as he imparts to us of his own Spirit, and at length takes such entire possession of the faculties of our souls, that it is no longer we who live and work, but it is Jesus who lives in and through us. His Spirit it is which possesses and impels us, and transforms us into real children of God. The humanity slain on the cross and vivified again, is the vehicle of this animating spirit of Christ, whereby we, according to the measure of our receptivity, really attain even to the fullness of God, which dwells bodily in Christ as the head of its body, and the highest brother-master of our order. However, this renovation of our humanity takes place only con ditionally and according to firmly fixed laws, not through a mere imputation without reality, without divine substance passing over from Jesus into our soul, but through a real, active, essential impartation of that Spirit who shall actuate us.   In order to become children of God, we must verily be born out of the *principium* in which it has pleased the Author of the whole to reveal himself as Father.   The Son must be essentially begotten out of the Father if he shall rightfully bear the name of son.   Who of you will affirm that the lower metals can be exalted to the degree of the earthly sun [*i. e.*, gold], without necessarily coming into real contact with the transmuting tincture? without being most intimately pervaded by it in all their particles?   *Now the flesh and blood of Jesus is the tincture for our souls as the earthly nature-savior is for the metals.*   Jesus was the first cross-brother who, through an essential union of Godhead and humanity, became *projectionable*, and prepared the panacea (*universalissimum*) for our souls.   Those twelve humble persons whom he chose as his apostles, with Mary his mother, and a few family connections, all gathered together in one mind and in hope of projection, were the first of Eve's children who yet in life were baptized with the Holy Ghost and received this vital tincture.   On the same day on which the Divine Spirit had formed so entirely novel kind of enthusiasts out of the apostles, that nearly every one was confounded by the circumstance, projection took place in three thousand persons; yea, and so gracious was the Lord, that from day to day he added more, so that in a short while the number of these happy children of light amounted to five thousand souls.   Since then the number of the faithful has grown to such a multitude, that John, who saw them in spirit, compares them to a band that no man could count; and in order that there may not be the least doubt that this multitude consists wholly of souls regenerated by the vital tincture of Jesus, John was instructed that these souls had all come out of great tribulation, and had washed their garments in the blood of the Lamb.*

Dear brother, we cannot too strongly and emphatically declare to you, that *the glorified flesh and blood of Jesus is the universal life-tincture of all humanity*, which has existed, exists, and will exist. Souls which, in the process of their regeneration, have already advanced so far that they have received this tincture in an especial measure, are then *medium-tinctures*, or genuine channels of projection, whereby Christ will gradually extend the reign of his Spirit over the whole surface of the earth. O children! for what mysteries would this subject afford us matter, if this were the place to pursue it to exhaustion. However, if you will meditate upon different matters that took place at your entrance into the Holy Order, and of which, both in our Decrees and in the genuine Order-tables, such far-glancing hints have been given, the blinding mist which has hitherto disturbed for you the true point of view, will be finally overpowered by the splendor of the truth, and will permit you to look without veil into the sanctuary of the Order. Gladly would we here, in help of your love of truth, still more draw back the curtain behind which lie hidden the jewels, *the treasures of both Lights ;* but we know too well how weak your shoulders still are, to dare openly to burden them with matters of such weight. Besides, it were all too perilous to exhibit the mysteries of Wisdom unveiled. What a sharp knife is in the hand of a child, such would be certain mysteries of the Order among brethren to whom is wanting the needful temper.

---

*Some readers may need to be informed, that, in the vocabulary of the Alchemists, the *powder or tincture of projection* was a certain powder or tincture cast into the *aludel*, or alembic, or other vessel full of some prepared metal, which is to be transmuted into *gold*, or of some prepared medicine, which is to be transmuted into a *panacea*. Any one interested may read a poetical account of the alchemical process in Goethe's "Faust:" see scene *Vor dem Thor*, the passage beginning
" *Mein Vater war ein dunkler Ehrenmann,*
Der uber die natur und ihre hail'gen kreise," &c.

APPENDIX F—2.

OTHER MEN HOLDING KINDRED VIEWS.

A further brief notice of the men referred to on page 96 as holding views similar to those of the Harmonists, may serve to show that they can claim respectable names as entertaining opinions not unlike to their own.

The mystical theology of Jacob Böhm has been sufficiently set forth in the preceding extracts from the *Hirten-Brief*, which although not written by Böhm himself, was the work of some one who was in full sympathy with his views.

J. GODFREY ARNOLD was an intimate friend of Spener, and was much admired and followed by the Pietists. In 1697, he was appointed Professor of History at Giessen, but he soon resigned, because, as he said, "no man can serve two masters," and professors, at that day, were required to teach in a manner that did not suit his taste. In 1700, on the recommendation of Franke, he was appointed court preacher to the Duchess of Isenach. In 1707, the King of Prussia made him pastor and inspector at Perleburg. He drank deep into the views of the mystics and pietists, and conceived high disgust with the reigning theology around him. He was an ingenuous and upright man ; but it is admitted that his strong prejudices may have warped his judgment as a historian.

His principal work was entitled "An Impartial History of the Church and of Heresies," in which he undertakes to defend most of those who were called heretics, against the accusations made against them by the orthodox. He made religion to consist very much in certain indescribable internal sensations and emotions, and had little regard for doctrinal theology. Mosheim seems to have had a very strong prejudice against him, and does not do him justice.

Kurtz, in his Church History, states that "he wrote and sang about the mysteries of the divine *Sophia*, when Adam, who was originally a *man-woman*, fell, and his female nature, the heavenly Sophia, was taken from him, and instead of it a carnal woman was formed out of his rib."

In Mosheim's and Schröckh's Church Histories, we have an account of JOHN WILLIAM PETERSEN, superintendent at Luneburg, who died in 1727. "He early gave way to a belief in visions and special revelations, which brought him to hold to a literal reign of Christ on the earth, during the millennium, and to believe in a final restoration of all things. He was undoubtedly a considerable scholar, and a very sincere and pious man. But his belief in dreams and visions led him to embrace very singular opinions, for which he also claimed the support of the Scriptures. He supposed that, prior to the millennium, the gospel would be preached over all the world, and that all nations would be converted. The Jews, after becoming Christians, would be restored to their own land. Then the first resurrection (that of the ancient saints and martyrs) would take place, Christ would appear in the clouds of heaven, and living saints would be caught up to meet the Lord in the air, and be changed. Thenceforth Christ would reign a thousand years on the earth, over a *two-fold church*—the celestial, composed of the risen saints, and those changed at his coming; and the terrestrial, embracing all other Christians. Religion would prevail very generally, but not universally. At the end of the thousand years Satan would be let loose; there would be a great apostasy; Christ would come forth and destroy the wicked; a new heaven and a new earth would appear, and gradually, all things would be restored to order, holiness, and happiness." He, and his wife, Joanna Eleanora, and Rosamond Juliana, a noble young lady, all claimed to have a sort of divine revelation, and " predicted a complete future restoration of all things, the liberation of both wicked men and devils from hell, their deliverance from all sin, and from the punishment of sin; and assigned to Christ a *two-fold human nature*—the one celestial and assumed before this world was created, the other, derived from his mother since the commencement of time. Many gave assent to these opinions, especially among the laity."

JOHN ALBERT BENGEL was born in 1868, in Würtemburg. He was distinguished for his learning and piety, and especially for his pioneer labors in the critical study of the New Testament. His Gnomon is a critical and practical commentary which has been translated into English, and is still highly valued for its deep spiritual insight into the meaning of the sacred text. He was orthodox in his theology, but of somewhat mystical tendencies. He condemned Zinzendorf and the Moravians for their sensuous views of the sufferings of Christ, and for placing the Son instead of the Father as the representative of the Trinity. He was a firm Millennarian, and published an Exposition of the Apocalypse, in which he fixed upon the year 1836 as the probable period of the great consummation. He also predicted in this work, that in the last ten years of the 18th century, the great conflict would commence, and the Romish throne be overturned. This was fulfilled in 1798, by the French occupation of Rome, and the deposition of the Pope by Napoleon; the fifth vial being thus " poured out on the seat of the beast," or temporal power of the Papacy.

HEINRICH JUNG STILLING, whose romantic Autobiography has been translated into English, and widely circulated both in Britain and in this country, is well known as a man of eminent piety and learning, of childlike simplicity of character, of most amiable spirit, and as one who impoverished himself by his gratuitous medical services and other labors, and charities for the benefit of the poor and suffering. Though a man of humble birth, he rose by successive steps, from the position of schoolmaster to that of physician and oculist, and then to that of Professor, and of Privy Counselor to the Grand Duke of Baden. He was mystico-pietistic in his religious views. He had great faith in the power of prayer, and did nothing without seeking divine direction. He regarded the spiritual world as not far removed from view, only thinly covered, and merely needing faith to have the veil withdrawn. Hence he was led in part to adopt the views of Swedenborg in regard to the possibility of perceiving and conversing with the spirits of the departed. He believed that those who leave this world in a state of imperfect holiness, have to remain in Hades until they are freed from all remaining impurity, before they are permitted to enter the heavenly state. He studied the Apocalypse much, and wrote a partial exposition of it, in which he also sought to fix the period of the great consummation. He wrote also a work in two volumes entitled " Scenes from the Invisible World," and another still more celebrated, in four volumes, which he called " Nostalgia" (Ger. *Heimweh* or Home Sickness), *heaven* being the home for which the weary pilgrim is longing. These works were written in 1793–4, and produced a profound sensation in the religious world; the latter especially, being very widely read in Europe, Asia, and America. They awakened anew in many pious souls a longing for *rest* in the heavenly home, from the fearful scenes of revolutionary strife with which Europe was then agitated. Many also were ready to welcome the second advent of Christ, to set up his glorious earthly kingdom, an event which they supposed to be near at hand.

OETINGER is another distinguished name which may be mentioned in this connection. He is called the great Swabian theosophist; a profound thinker, concerning whom Schubart has said that an academy of learning expired with him. He endeavored to develop the entire system of theology from the idea of Life. There is in his writings a mixture of the mystico-speculative tendency of Böhm with the pietistico-practical of Spener. He favored somewhat the visionary notions of Swedenborg. He appears to have had an influence in shaping the opinions of Michael Hahn, who was for a time a collaborator with George Rapp, as noticed in our first chapter, p. 26.

This MICHAEL HAHN is mentioned by Kurtz in his Church History as having given rise to a party or sect of followers who were named from him *Michelianer* (Michelians or Michelites). This sect he says " arose in Würtemburg as a secondary or after-effect of Spenerian pietism impregnated by the theosophy of Oetinger. Its founder was a layman, Michael Hahn, a butcher by trade; which, however, gave place to an extensive ministry in spiritual things. He died in 1819. His writings are full of deep glances into the divine economy of salvation; among which his "Letters on the Revelation of God through the whole Creation, &c." are especially worthy of mention. His peculiar doctrines were, that of a two-fold Fall (from which followed by inference, a great contempt for, though not rejection of the married state); that of the restoration of all things; further, and before all, the disparagement of justification in comparison with sanctification, of Christ *for us* in comparison with Christ *in us*; and finally, insistence upon continued repentance." He was a man of some learning, and besides a number of hymns of considerable merit, he wrote a commentary on portions of the New Testament, in the form of letters to his people, in three volumes. This work is in possession of the Harmonists.

APPENDIX G.

(See page 43.)

GEORGE RAPP ON HIS DEATH-BED.

THE following memorandum has been furnished since most of this volume was in type, by one who watched with him during the last night of his life:

"His strong faith in the literal fulfilment of the promises concerning the personal coming of Jesus Christ, and the gathering of the whole of Israel (as foretold Luke 21 : 24-27, Rom. 11 : 25, Jer. chaps. 31, 32, 33, &c.), remained unshaken to his last moments, as was shown by his last words, when he felt the strong gripe of the hand of approaching death, saying : 'If I did not so fully believe, that the Lord has designed me to place our Society before his presence in the land of Canaan, I would consider this my last.' In 1844 and 1845, there was a very lively revival in the Society, which he considered a sure sign of the nearness of the long hoped for event. For a number of years he kept everything in readiness which the Society would have needed for the journey to the land of Israel."

This belief, on his own part, will readily explain why many of his people could not be brought to believe that Father Rapp would die before the Lord's coming. The Lord did indeed COME to call his servant home, but not in the way he expected. Some of them still look for him to return and be their leader when the Lord shall appear.